Washington, DC

Berlitz Publishing Company, Inc.
Princeton   Mexico City   London   Eschborn   Singapore

Original Text:	Martin Gostelow
Photography:	Jay Fechtman, except Erling Mandelmann pages 34, 67, 100; page 73 courtesy of USHMM Photo Archives
Cover Photo:	Jay Fechtman
Photo Editor:	Naomi Zinn
Layout:	Media Content Marketing, Inc.
Cartography:	Ortelius Design

*Although the publisher tries to insure the accuracy of all the infor-
mation in this book, changes are inevitable and errors may result.
The publisher cannot be responsible for any resulting loss, incon-
venience, or injury. If you find an error in this guide, please let the
editors know by writing to Berlitz Publishing Company, 400
Alexander Park, Princeton, NJ 08540-6306.*

ISBN 2-8315-7823-X

Printed in Italy
020/111 RP

Washington, DC

THE CITY AND ITS PEOPLE

Washington, DC, although not within one of the 50 United States, is truly the all-American city. In the best sense of the word, the nation's capital belongs to the people, who look upon it as half-shrine, half fun-fair, and as such it has long been one of the most popular family vacation spots in the country. No visitor should miss this uniquely American experience.

In climate and flavor Washington is Southern, for it lies south of the Mason-Dixon Line, the boundary between Pennsylvania and Maryland that had traditionally separated the North from "Dixie," the South. It was the first modern city built from scratch to be a national capital. In 1790 George Washington himself picked the spot for the "Federal City" that was to bear his name, and laid the cornerstone of the Capitol; but he died before Congress first met here, in 1800. Virginia and Maryland ceded parts of their state territory along the Potomac River for the site set aside as the District of Columbia—"DC."

Broad avenues radiating like spokes from the Capitol and White House are lined with government buildings designed to impress. The architectural styles adopted over two centuries are a mirror of changing official taste, from Greek and Roman to contemporary steel and glass. Happily, the scale is human —there are no skyscrapers or disfiguring industrial installations here—and the setting is verdant, with open spaces, parks, fountains, and countless monuments. If all this seems reminiscent of Paris, there is good reason. The man who laid out the plans for Washington, DC, Pierre Charles L'Enfant, himself a Frenchman, was inspired by memories of Paris.

Some of the monuments are both beautiful and central to American history. Preeminent is the Lincoln Memorial; the great seated statue of Abraham Lincoln, surrounded by the

Dupont Circle is the center of a bustling Washington neighborhood, great for shopping or just hanging out.

words of the Gettysburg Address, which many American school-children learn by heart, symbolizes the healed trauma of the Civil War. It faces the spot where Martin Luther King, Jr. made his "I Have a Dream" address to civil rights marchers demanding fulfillment of Lincoln's ideals. Beyond the memorial's Reflecting Pool, the Washington Monument spears the clouds through a ring of flags. Nearby, cherry blossom trees (they don't yield cherries) that were a gift from Japan encircle the Potomac's Tidal Basin and the classic white marble temple dedicated to Thomas Jefferson, author of the Declaration of Independence. These spacious vistas are grand without being grandiose.

Washington manages to combine the educational with the entertaining. Families with kids in tow line up to see

CONTENTS

● A ( in the text denotes a highly recommended sight

Ford's Theater, where Lincoln was assassinated; the exhibits from famous crimes at the Federal Bureau of Investigation (FBI); George Washington's wooden false teeth at Mt. Vernon; and the animals at the zoo. More lines form at the Air and Space Museum's exciting displays. Other offshoots of the Smithsonian Institution house a treasure trove of milestones gleaned from what might arguably be called the American century.

Visitors fill the magnificent National Gallery of Art; they line up to see the original Shakespeare folios in the Folger Library, the Declaration of Independence at the National Archives, and the Gutenberg Bible at the Library of Congress; and they attend the concerts and stage productions at the Kennedy Center. They wander among the dogwood trees in the gardens of Dumbarton Oaks, take the White House tour, and cluster in the rotunda under the Capitol dome.

Some landmarks are somber. The Vietnam Veterans Memorial's stark wall covered with the names of the dead makes no pretense of glorifying their sacrifice. Its statement is moving, a personal and collective sorrow for families and the nation. Many visitors have tears in their eyes here, as they may also at President Kennedy's grave on the hillside overlooking Arlington National Cemetery's acres of graves.

Most Washingtonians work for the government—the federal payroll is 300,000 and growing, despite promises of less bureaucracy from every presidential candidate. They come from every state in the Union, are relatively young, and there's a higher-than-average percentage of single women. For fun they go to the bars and restaurants of Adams Morgan and Georgetown. The latter, an elegant residential district founded in 1665 and incorporated into DC, is noted for its shady streets lined with Georgian houses contemporary with those in Dublin. Today, these are the homes of the capital's movers and shakers. Washington is also home to a number of leading colleges and universities, which add to the city's vibrant social scene. They also contribute to the ethnic diversity that is evident in the Washington DC community.

In Washington, there's always something new or surprising going on. Someone stands for hours shouting protests at the front door of the FBI building and no one bats an eye. Someone else camps in a plastic tent 20 yards from the White House to air a grievance. See how different people surface at different times of day: dawn commuter; Mom or Dad on the school run; neatly packaged young executive, trained to radiate confidence; conventioneer with name badge; tourist family; boisterous school outing; pedigree Georgetown dowager walking a pedigree dog; after-work happy-hour gang; restaurant crowd; and real night owls, all a part of the colorful local tapestry.

After a trip to Washington, DC, Americans return home feeling patriotic and edified. Foreign visitors leave with a sense of astonished discovery. Behind the Washington of the headlines, they find a city of beauty, dignity, and spectacular attractions.

Look for the name of a lost loved one at the Vietnam Veteran's Memorial.

A BRIEF HISTORY

The idea of a purpose-built capital city is not so strange now. But it must have seemed wildly visionary in 1790, when Congress authorized the newly elected President Washington to select a site "not exceeding 10 miles square" on the Potomac River.

In the early years after American independence, Congress was more or less nomadic, convening in Philadelphia, Baltimore, Annapolis, New York, and several other cities. When a statue of George Washington was commissioned in 1783, Francis Hopkinson, one of the signatories of the Declaration of Independence, suggested that it be put on wheels so that it could follow Congress about. Philadelphia might well have become the legislators' permanent home but, in the same year, soldiers demanding back pay stormed a session of Congress there and the next meeting was prudently held in Princeton.

By this time, members from Southern states resented what they saw as excessive Northern influence; Northerners hated the prospect of a long journey to some Southern city. The North, however, had run up far greater debts in the independence struggle, so Thomas Jefferson, then Secretary of State, and Treasury Secretary Alexander Hamilton—rarely in accord—agreed to deliver the votes of their respective followers for a quid pro quo. If Congress were to take over the states' debts, the capital would be located as far south as the Potomac, with the exact place to be decided by George Washington himself.

Choosing the Site

Washington opted for the full 10 by 10 miles (16 by 16 km), in a diamond shape mostly on the Maryland bank but including some of the Virginia side of the river. (That piece went back to Virginia in 1846, destroying the symmetry.) Given the

Return to the early twentieth century in the former home of the 28th president of the United States, Woodrow Wilson.

terms of the deal, it's clear why Washington chose this area. It included Alexandria, nearest town to his beloved estate of Mount Vernon; it incorporated Georgetown, at the furthest point that seagoing ships could reach on the Potomac. The new capital territory could have its own port, which was considered essential. There were already plans to cut a canal to bypass the river's rapids and offer a trade route with lands opening up to the west. Commissioners were appointed for this "Territory of Columbia" (the even less romantic word "District" crept in later), and it was they who simply announced the capital's name: the City of Washington.

Thinking Big

The backdrop for the first president's inauguration in New York had been designed by a talented French engineer, Pierre Charles L'Enfant, a veteran of the Revolutionary War. Washington was obviously impressed, because he appointed the young officer to come up with a proposal for the layout of the new city. L'Enfant surveyed the unpromising terrain and produced a staggeringly ambitious scheme. Although a population of 8,000 was big in those days (only six cities in the new United States exceeded it), he dreamed of an eventual 800,000.

L'Enfant's plan used slight rises in the ground to settle the President's House and the Congress House at either end of a broad avenue, since named Pennsylvania. That didn't just make for a good view, it kept them out of the mud—a lot of this area was notoriously swampy. The two buildings would be the focal points for more avenues radiating from them. On a third low hill, where the present Washington Monument stands, there was to have been a statue of Washington on horseback. East and north of this basic triangle, the area would be filled in with a grid of streets.

The Frenchman set to work in 1791—and ran straight into trouble. People were building wooden houses and huts where he demanded grand vistas. Bitter arguments blew up between the hot-tempered "L'Enfant Terrible" and those who thought free Americans ought to be able to build where they liked—some of whom had influence in high places. Only a year after he had begun, his disagreements with the commissioners had become so violent that the president felt compelled to dismiss him. It was a tragedy for the engineer and for the city, though mercifully many of the elements of L'Enfant's vision survived in the years that followed.

Work began on a mansion for the president, and Washington laid the cornerstone of the Capitol in 1793. Progress was slow, but by 1800 there were enough small offices for all 126 government officials to move from Philadelphia. The Congress was able to meet in the completed wing of the Capitol and John Adams could move into the White House for the end of his term as second president, although it was damp

Arlington National Cemetery is a grave reminder of the thousands of Americans lost in defense of their country.

and far from finished, according to his wife Abigail. Others fared no better: the number of substantial houses in the city did not reach double figures.

In 1801, Jefferson became the first president to take the oath of office in Washington, in a ceremony deliberately devoid of ostentation. The new century generated new ambitions for the nation, but its capital was to be shamefully neglected. L'Enfant's "city of magnificent distances" was scorned as a "capital of miserable huts" and a "mud-hole" by members of the Congress. Carping voices never ceased suggesting that the capital should shift to somewhere else: fortunately, there was no consensus as to which place.

The British Light a Fire

War with Britain came again in 1812. In retaliation for American attacks on Canada, a British force under Admiral Cockburn landed in Maryland and occupied Washington. On 24

August 1814, the invaders set fire to the White House and other federal buildings, including the two completed wings of the Capitol. The buildings were gutted, but a torrent of rainfall that night luckily limited the damage—but not before the White House had turned decidedly black. Everyone had to find temporary accommodations, but at least indignation at the wicked British brought about a patriotic feeling for the capital. Agitation to find another site went out of fashion, though only the advent of railroads and the telegraph finally killed it off. Forty years of haphazard growth followed, with the addition of a few large buildings but scarcely any amenities.

Civil War Capital

The 1850s saw the long-simmering pot of North-South division and resentment come to a boil. The South, fearing interference with the institution of slavery, insisted on states' rights vis à vis the Union. The North was determined to prevent slavery from spreading into new states that were forming in the territories of the west. Rancor in Congress turned from verbal to actual physical violence. In October 1859, the abolitionist John Brown raided Harpers Ferry, Virginia, calling on all slaves to revolt. He was hanged for treason, but hailed by many in the North as a martyr. In the 1860 elections, the Democrats split between North and South and the pro-Union Republican candidate Abraham Lincoln was elected president entirely on votes from the Northern states. The South seceded and formed the Confederate States of America. All-out war ensued, and Washington, on the border between Union and Confederate forces, was the focus—both politically and geographically.

The Civil War was sparked when South Carolina troops fired on the federal base at Fort Sumter on 12 April 1861. Opposing armies were quickly formed around Washington and the Confederate capital of Richmond, Virginia, only about 100 miles (160 km) to the south. Most people thought it would soon be over, but the nightmare lasted four years. By the end, 600,000 had died in combat, either of wounds or from disease. Union forces tried to take Richmond several times, and Confederates tried twice to break into the North just inland from Washington, so some of the greatest battles took place around the city. At times even the Capitol was used as a hospital for the wounded. Government departments proliferated and more desks were squeezed in wherever they would fit. The population of the capital doubled between 1861 and 1865, suddenly including 40,000 freed slaves. At last, the North's preponderance in population and industry began to prevail over the South's superior military leadership. The Southern hero, Robert E. Lee, his forces outnumbered and surrounded and with Richmond lost, surrendered to Ulysses S. Grant on 9 April 1865. Just five days later, Lincoln was assassinated at Ford's Theater in Washington by a Confederate sympathizer.

In 1871, Ulysses S. Grant, then president, appointed a new city government for DC, and its administrator, Alexander "Boss" Shepherd, set about providing the roads, street lights, and sewers that had been lacking for so long. Countless trees were planted in the first of several beautification programs in Washington's history. In the process, the budget was overspent many times and Congress resumed control, but at least the work was done. L'Enfant's plan turned up again in 1887, and in 1909 he was reburied with honors in Arlington National Cemetery. Civic and national pride in the city increased. People began to visit, to view the monuments and witness the documents that told the story of the birth of the United States.

Growth, Depression, and a New Deal

World War I led to another huge increase in the bureaucracy. Temporary office buildings (that remained for decades) disfigured the Mall. Between the wars, foreign diplomats regarded Washington as a hardship post, a somnolent backwater lacking any finesse of culture or cuisine. The depression that followed the Wall Street Crash of 1929 brought hunger-marchers and a "Bonus Army" of war veterans to camp near the White House. When some refused to leave, they were driven out by the army with tanks and tear gas. Franklin D. Roosevelt became president in 1933 with the promise of a New Deal to create employment by a huge program of public works. That, of course, meant many more jobs in the federal government, as well as for the lobbyists and lawyers that circle it like pilot fish around a whale. When 1941 brought the US into World War II, payrolls escalated again and buildings went up with amazing speed. The world's largest office building, the Pentagon, took only 18 months to build and housed over 28,000 war planners.

The Navy Memorial pays homage to the brave men and women who have sailed the Seven Seas.

Transformation

Victory was followed by the Cold War and the McCarthy witch-hunts for real and imaginary communists. In 1954, the Supreme Court ruled against racial segregation in public (state) schools, and the capital was the first to comply. A plan mounted to build the Kennedy Center was meant to repair Washington's cultural deficiencies, though it would be many years before the complex was finished. The president it honored and his successor, Lyndon B. Johnson, campaigned for a better city. Meanwhile, Martin Luther King, Jr. inspired the struggle of African Americans for the rights they had been promised a century before. His assassination in 1968 triggered the riots that ruined much of the old downtown area and set it back a decade.

The people of DC gradually gained—or regained—most of the democratic rights of "normal" US citizens over this period. They could at last vote in a presidential election, then for a Representative in Congress (though still not one with a full vote). In 1975, they could vote again for a city council and mayor. There is a movement afoot to make DC a state, so that it can also be represented in the Senate. The year 1976 saw celebrations for the bicentennial of the Declaration of Independence—and the opening of the first Metro line. More trees and gardens than ever were planted and now flourish. Decaying downtown areas are being renewed, with the Convention Center as a flagship. Fine old buildings were saved and fresh uses were found for them. Union Station was renovated and now offers a variety of shopping and eating choices to the train traveler. New museums and galleries have almost completed the lines along the Mall. Today, ceremonial and cultural Washington looks better than ever.

WHERE TO GO

Fortunately, most of Washington's sights are concentrated in one part of the city. Practically all are in a rectangle extending from the Lincoln Memorial and the Watergate complex in the west to the Library of Congress and Union Station in the east. Georgetown, northwest of this area, Dupont Circle, north of the White House, and Arlington, south across the Potomac, are easily accessible. Although the Metro system conveniently links most attractions, there is also a system of Tourmobile shuttle buses connecting many monuments and museums, and you can get on and off as many times as you like with a day ticket. Guides provide cheerful commentaries as you ride. Everywhere, it pays to make an early start, if only to arrive before the school groups.

THE WHITE HOUSE

(1600 Pennsylvania Avenue, NW) Can thousands of people a day walk through any other family's home, let alone that of the head of a great nation? Visits are limited to 10am–noon Tuesday–Saturday, White House business permitting. From September through March, no ticket is needed (excluding the busy Christmas season); visitors line up at the White House East Gate on Executive Avenue. In spring and summer, free, same-day, timed tickets must be obtained from the White House Visitors' Center (1450 Pennsylvania Avenue; Tel. 202-208-1631). Be early: In peak season, the daily allocation may run out by 8:30am. Individuals are allowed up to four tickets. US citizens who plan ahead (three months or more) can get a ticket for a special tour before 10am by writing to one of their Congressional representatives.

If the White House looks just right to us now, that may be because it is such a familiar image, an icon to represent the country. Pierre L'Enfant chose its site, at the other end of his broad avenue (now Pennsylvania) from the Capitol. The sweeping view L'Enfant envisaged between the two buildings was marred in 1836, when President Andrew Jackson sited the Treasury Building next door to the White House.

Thomas Jefferson suggested they hold a national competition to design the "President's House" (the actual name, the White House, already in use as a nickname before 1814, was not officially recognized by Congress till 1902) and put in an anonymous entry himself, which looked rather like his Monticello. It was beaten by a proposal from Irish-born James Hoban for the kind of mansion the gentry were building near Dublin at the time. The new house wasn't finished soon enough for Washington to live in; his successor John Adams only had four months of his term left when he moved in. Jefferson then spent eight years here, and, though he said it was "big enough for two emperors, one Pope, and the Grand Lama," proceeded to add east and west terraces and pavilions. Later, just about every president made improvements. James Madison needed to order a complete reconstruction of the White House after the British set fire to it in the raid of 1814.

By 1948, when Mrs. Truman noticed the legs of the piano sinking into the floor and chandeliers shaking dangerously when anyone walked overhead, investigations showed that the long-suffering White House had taken all the piecemeal additions and tinkering it could stand. It had to be totally rebuilt. But the interiors, right down to the plaster, were painstakingly removed, stored, and later put back in place.

Tours enter through the **East Wing** lobby, after security checks. From the **Garden Room**, with its Chinese-style furniture of the early 19th century, look out into the Jacqueline Kennedy Garden. As you walk along the corridor lined with portraits of former first ladies, you may be able to glance into

Perhaps the most recognized American address, 1600 Pennsyvania Avenue has had a long list of tenants.

some of the rooms leading off: the Library, the China Room, the Vermeil Room (named for the collection of gilded silver it holds), and the elegant oval Diplomatic Reception Room with French wallpaper of 1834 printed with American scenes.

Back near the lobby, you climb the stairs to the right, just like any guest invited to a state reception, to the sparkling gold-and-white **East Room**. The first first lady to live here, Abigail Adams, who hung out the laundry in this room, would scarcely recognize it today. Largest in the White House, it's where presidential press conferences, concerts, and the weddings of presidents' daughters are held. The color scheme was chosen by Mrs. Theodore Roosevelt—her husband liked to stage boxing matches here, and their children were allowed to rollerskate or ride their ponies inside when the weather was bad. The 1796 portrait of George Washington by Gilbert Stuart is the one saved by Dolly Madison from the fire-raising British in 1814.

The **Green Room** next-door was Jefferson's dining room, where he liked to surprise his guests with new eating experiences such as ice cream, waffles, and macaroni. Since his day it has been a parlor or sitting room, and was President Kennedy's favorite. A Martin portrait shows Benjamin Franklin with a bust of his hero, Isaac Newton. John and Abigail Adams were painted by Gilbert Stuart.

The **Blue Room**, like those above and below it, is oval, making use of the curved south portico. (The president's famous Oval Office, however, is in the West Wing, and is not on view to the public.) The gilded chairs and sofa were ordered from Paris in 1817 by James Monroe. A row of presidential portraits decorates the walls. The room has mainly been used for receiving guests.

In the **Red Room**, the walls are of deep red silk. The portraits include one of John James Audubon, the naturalist and artist, here dressed in buckskin.

The **State Dining Room** seems quite austere after those rich colors, and modestly sized, but it can seat 140. The George Healy portrait of Lincoln, reckoned to be one of the best likenesses of him, was painted from photographs and memory (the artist only saw Lincoln once).

Unless invited by the president and his family, you won't see the second and third floors where the family and guest apartments are situated, including the Queen's Bedroom, where several royal visitors have slept; Winston Churchill moved himself here during his stay because he didn't like the Lincoln Bedroom—or Lincoln's bed.

On the way out, you pass through **Cross Hall**, with portraits of recent presidents. Then you exit through the marbled lobby and north portico, which is your chance at last to get a photograph of "me at the White House." (It beats the "me and cardboard cut-outs of the president and first lady" pictures that you can pose for in the street.) Walk around the outside of the fence to see the best-loved exterior view, across the south lawn, where the presidential helicopter takes off.

Around the White House

With the massive Greek-revival bulk of the Treasury already on one side (the east), the White House collected another neighbor on the other (west) side, though it took 17 years to build (1871–1888). Ever since the Civil War, expanded government departments had been housed all over the city in crowded temporary accommodations. The plan was to cure the problem at a stroke, with the biggest office building ever built up to that time. Now labeled the **Old Executive Office Building**, it's been called the "greatest monstrosity in America" (by President Truman, and he meant this as praise) and hailed as a national treasure. It was the style that so horrified many critics. They'd expected another Greek temple, but they got a hunk of French Second Empire that matched, though it dwarfed, only the Renwick Gallery across Pennsylvania Avenue. Every loving piece of decorative detail that could be put into it, was. Long the home of the War, Navy, and State departments, the O.E.O.B. now houses some of the White House staff, the Vice-President's Office, and the National Security Council. Even so, you can get inside on Saturday mornings, if you call in advance for a tour reservation (Tel. 202-395-5895). If you have any interest in architecture or the decorative arts, go. The three libraries are jewels of Victoriana, now that the shamefaced wraps have been taken off them and they've been restored to their original splendor.

Across Pennsylvania Avenue from the O.E.O.B., the Blair and Lee houses are for V.I.P. guests of the president; **Blair House**

Although it looks like a palace, the Old Executive Office Building is actually host to a bevy of governmental offices.

was where the Trumans lived while the White House was being reconstructed. In the **Lee House**, Robert E. Lee was offered the command of the Union army at the outbreak of the Civil War. The **Renwick Gallery** (1859) has displays of the best in American craft and design and related temporary exhibitions. The building itself is worth seeing for its lush Grand Salon and Octagon Room and their appropriate 19th-century paintings— sentimental, romantic, and mildly erotic. It was built to house the Corcoran collection, but when that grew too big it had to be moved a couple of blocks down 17th Street to a new white marble **Corcoran Gallery of Art** in 1897 (see page 65).

Lafayette Square faces the north side of the White House. Its green lawns are a traditional gathering place for demonstrators hoping to make a point with the president— or the media. Huge groups assemble for an hour or two, and eccentric individualists or the homeless sleep under tents of plastic sheet. The bronze horseman in the middle is Andrew Jackson, not Lafayette—he's in a corner.

At the northwest corner, Commodore Stephen Decatur, a naval hero of the War of 1812, had a new house built, the first on the square. In 1819, he and his wife moved in, but after little more than a year he was dead, killed in a duel with a rival officer. Designed by Benjamin Latrobe, the **Decatur House** was later let to foreign ambassadors and US secretaries of state. Now it's a museum with fine antiques and some of Decatur's possessions.

On the north side of the square, **St. John's Church** (1815) is another Latrobe design; almost every president since it was built has attended once, if not regularly. It was considered the most fashionable church in the city. At one time, you actually had to pay rent for your pew. If you take a look inside, you will see the elegant white interior, the stained glass by a curator from Chartres, and the presidential Pew 54.

Washington, DC was still a village of scattered huts and muddy tracks in 1798, when George Washington persuaded his friend Colonel John Tayloe to set an example and build a town house here instead of in Philadelphia. He chose a plot on the corner of 18th Street and New York Avenue, and William Thornton, first architect of the Capitol, designed the **Octagon** for him. However, someone couldn't count—there are only six sides instead of eight. President Madison moved in here after the British burned the White House. (They'd have burned the Octagon too, but it had become the French Embassy.) He signed the Treaty of Ghent that ended the War of 1812 in the elegant circular room over the entrance hall.

Back on 17th Street, after the Corcoran Gallery you'll pass more white marble, the Greek-style American Red Cross building, and then, at 1776 (no coincidence) D Street, the headquarters of the **Daughters of the American Revolution**. Imposing name; imposing Classical temple. The D.A.R., as they are usually called, are ladies descended from anyone who campaigned for American independence. They keep a museum of period rooms from different eras and states, but they're mostly known to the public for their 4,000-seat assembly hall, Washington's best for concerts until the Kennedy Center was finished.

Finally, as you reach the Mall, take a look at the 1910 **O.A.S. Building** (the Organization of American States). Here, you will be able to see a juxtaposition of North- and South-American motifs—Aztec, Maya, and Inca, and reliefs of Washington, Bolívar, and San Martín.

THE MALL

This is a perfect piece of theater. Stand on the steps of the Lincoln Memorial and look along 2 miles (3 km) of magnificent green, 500 yards (442 m) wide, to the shining white dome of the Capitol. Enough runners for a mass marathon head in all directions and at every speed. People picnic, fly kites, and throw Frisbees. Weekends see friendly soccer, rugby, and softball matches. High school marching bands assemble for parades, buses decant eager tourists. This arena, the Mall, is faced by some of the world's most wonderful museums and galleries.

If the Mall today is a delight, for much of the 19th century it was still a mud heap, with piles of rubbish and swampy pools. The Baltimore & Ohio Railroad built tracks across it about where the National Gallery of Art now stands. "Temporary" buildings from both world wars lingered more than twenty years after the second was over. Some of the Mall had been paved over for parking lots. It was only gradually that it all began to come right. Presidents Kennedy and Johnson battled for the beautification of the city. The debris was swept away, far more trees were planted, and major cross-streets went underground. The result is not quite Pierre

The symbol of Washington DC is the towering Washington Monument, shown here in a glowing sunset silhouette.

Charles L'Enfant's dream come true; he had hoped for an American Champs-Elysées, lined with great mansions and embassies. But the spirit is true to his vision.

The majestic white marble **Washington Monument** is the focal point of the Mall and symbol of the city. It is unimaginable that anything else could stand in the place of this 555-ft (169-m) obelisk, which perfectly embodies the nobility of George Washington himself and shines like a beacon to lead the nation. How many lost visitors, too, must have been saved by the sight of it. There's usually a line waiting to go up in the elevator, except possibly at the summer opening time of 8am, or on summer evenings, when the monument is open until midnight. Despite the small windows, the view from the top is superb. The Monument has recently undergone a sweeping interior and exterior renovation, and though the 897 stairs are now closed to the public, the rest of the interior is open for tours.

The monument nearly didn't turn out this way. After a competition in 1833, the winning design by Robert Mills showed a decorated obelisk rising from a circular colonnaded building, adorned with statues. It would have looked like a single candle on a birthday cake. Fortunately, tight budgets cut out the cake and left the candle. Funds were raised by public subscription, and work started on a simple obelisk in 1848. By 1854, political squabbling brought it to a stop at 160 feet (49 m) up and there it stayed for 25 years. In 1880, the Army's engineers were called in to finish the job, which they did, by 1884. You can see a slight change of color in the marble at the point where work was resumed. The first elevator, steam-driven, took 12 minutes to reach the top; the present one takes only 70 seconds.

West of the Washington Monument, walk the tree-lined path by a 2,000-ft- (609-m-) long reflecting pool to the **Lincoln Memorial**, a Classical temple inspired by the Parthenon. Visitors here bring much in expectation and receive as much in inspiration. The 16th president, deemed savior of the Union and martyred at the very point of victory in the Civil War, is uniquely esteemed; his memorial is revered as no other. It's an extraordinary amalgam of architecture, sculpture, and literature. Congress wrangled and dithered for 50 years, but at last the site was selected ("dignified isolation from competing structures" was specified—and achieved magnificently). Swamp-land had to be drained and a mound created. By 1922 the memorial was finished, and the wait had been worthwhile.

In Henry Bacon's design, 36 Doric columns represent the states of the Union at the time of Lincoln's death. The 19-ft (5.8-m) seated white marble statue of Lincoln inside took Daniel Chester French 13 years to carve. It seems to fill the chamber, but the air is one of compassion and contemplation, not power. Only the clenched left hand conveys tension. If you can, come here in the early light of the morning and again at night. The dramatic floodlighting was an afterthought; sheets of marble in the roof, oiled with paraffin to make them translucent, didn't give enough emphasis to Lincoln's face.

On the walls of the interior, Lincoln's famous words, with the power and emotional resonance of great and familiar music, are inscribed. To the right of the entrance, the Second Inaugural Address: "With malice toward none; with charity for all; with firmness in the right..." To the left, the Gettysburg Address: "...that this nation under God shall have a new birth of freedom—and that government of the people, by the people, for the people shall not perish from the earth."

Not far to the northeast, in Constitution Gardens, is a much newer place of pilgrimage, the **Vietnam Veterans Memorial**. Doubtful of it at first, Americans have now taken it to their hearts and visit it in the millions. The V-shaped wall of polished black granite, like a cut in the earth, bears the names of the more than 58,000 soldiers who died or remain missing. Beside each perfectly etched name (inscribed in order of their death or disappearance), a small cross indicates one of the missing, a diamond someone whose death was confirmed.

A group of veterans themselves campaigned for a memorial to be built, and in 1980 Congress agreed on the site. A competition for the design brought 1,421 entries, judged anonymously. The

Contemplate the somber visage of Abraham Lincoln.

winner, remarkably, was a 21-year-old student at Yale, Maya Ying Lin, whose parents had emigrated to the US from China. "The names would become the memorial," she said, and there is no other inscription.

Already touching traditions have grown around the 247-ft (75-m) wall of Indian granite. Relations and loved ones leave mementoes: toys, messages, photographs, and badges. Everything is collected by the Park Rangers, and, with the exception of flowers and unmarked flags, items are catalogued and kept in a museum storeroom. People make rubbings of the names with wax pencils. Everyone touches the mirror-smooth surface.

The message conveyed by the monument is achingly sad, befitting such a controversial war. Disappointed, some veterans demanded a more traditional commemoration. Soon after the wall's dedication in 1982, the Memorial Fund was urged to add the figurative sculpture and flagstaff that now

Korean War veterans have been memorialized in this active figurative sculpture located on the Mall.

stand nearby. Frederick Hart's realistic group of three young fighting men was unveiled in 1984.

In front of the Lincoln Memorial, adjacent to the Reflecting Pool, is the **Korean War Veterans Memorial**. Dedicated in 1995, the memorial features stainless steel sculptures of 19 life-size, heavily armed soldiers marching in the direction of an American flag. A black granite wall, inscribed with the words "Freedom Is Not Free," is etched with 2,500 images of nurses, chaplains, crew chiefs, mechanics, and other support troops who served in the conflict. A circular reflecting pool, a flag rising out of the center, is nearby. It is intended to be a living memorial, honoring all those who made it home as well as the 55,000 American troops who did not.

The Capitol

(Capitol Hill) At the east end of the Mall, the ground rises gently to a low hill—Capitol Hill. L'Enfant called it "a pedestal waiting for a monument." There, just where he intended, stands the majestic Capitol, or "Congress House," as he named it on his plan. Each of the 50 state capitals has a Capitol, too; if you confuse the two words, you'll only be doing the same as many Americans. Crowning its elevated site, Washington's Capitol is a landmark visible from most places in the city and even from points beyond the distant Beltway.

The original design for the Capitol was submitted by a gifted amateur, Dr. William Thornton, and in an obvious recipe for future friction, the runner-up in the competition was appointed to supervise construction. George Washington himself laid the cornerstone in 1793. Thornton's drawings showed a low flattish dome, but as the building was enlarged to keep pace with the growing nation, a taller and grander affair of wood and copper sheeting was built. National aspirations then demanded the still more impressive Baroque version that you see now, inspired by St. Peter's in Rome and Les Invalides in Paris, and over 4,000 tons of cast iron—a revolutionary use of the material for the time—were hauled into place between 1851 and 1863. Architect Thomas Walter was helped by the indefatigable Montgomery C. Meigs and his US Army engineers, who later finished off the Washington Monument and built the fine Old Pension Building. It was suggested to Lincoln during the depths of the Civil War that construction should stop and wait for peace, but he demurred: "If the people see the Capitol going on, it is a sign we intend the Union shall go on."

Placed atop the dome in 1863, the 19-ft (5.8-m) statue of Freedom very nearly didn't make it. The American sculptor Thomas Crawford's first drawings showed the lady in the kind of cap worn by freed Roman slaves and French revolutionaries. Jefferson Davis, then in Lincoln's first cabinet, regarded this as an incitement to Southern slaves to rebel, so Crawford changed it to a strange plumed helmet. He worked in Rome, so he sent a plaster model of his creation by sea—and shortly afterwards died. The ship was caught in a storm and as it was in danger of sinking, a lot of the cargo was thrown overboard. Not Freedom. She was still there when the ship limped into harbor at Bermuda to be scrapped; she eventually reached Washington where a bronze casting was made. Seemingly wrapped in a bedspread and bristling with lightning conductors, she's better seen from afar, up on her lofty perch, which, incidentally, moves in small circles as the heat of the sun expands the great iron dome.

The entrance to the Capitol is on the east side. The north wing houses the Senate and the south the House of Representatives. The whole ensemble looks so familiar and right that it's hard

*The massive Baroque dome of the easily recognizable
Capitol building is the crown jewel of the Washington skyline.*

to believe that it resulted from the piecemeal expansion plans of many architects. The last, in 1960–1962, substituted a new central portico and steps, the ones you climb now.

People used to wander freely throughout the vast building —and in many areas they still can, after a security check at the entrance, (note the massive bronze doors cast in Munich in 1861) though a 1998 shooting off the top of the Rotunda raised some understandable concerns about security. You arrive first in the vast **Rotunda**, 180 ft (55 m) from floor to ceiling and 96 ft (29 m) across. Tours of the building lasting about 45 minutes start frequently from here, and while you're waiting, your eyes will certainly be drawn to the painting up in the dome. It's a rather weird fresco, *The Apotheosis of George Washington,* which might well have embarrassed the subject. The artist, Italian-born Constantino Brumidi, settled in the United States

and painted in the Capitol for 25 years. He finished this picture in 11 months in 1865, using the technique of applying paint to wet plaster as Michelangelo did for the Sistine Chapel in Rome— though the result is less highly regarded. It shows Washington in the center, glorified by Liberty and Victory and surrounded by 13 robed maidens representing the original 13 states of the

Docent tours of the Rotunda provide information about the Revolutionary period.

Union. Around the rim, various allegorical groups include Minerva, goddess of wisdom, with Benjamin Franklin and Samuel Morse (inventor of the code). Armed Freedom, below Washington, is a portrait of the artist's wife.

In 1877, when Brumidi was already 72, he started on the 300-ft- (91-m-) long monochrome frieze which runs round the wall of the Rotunda about 60 ft (18 m) up. Also in fresco, though imitating sculpture, it shows scenes from American history, starting with Columbus. Only about one-third was complete when the artist had a fall while painting. Not all the way down, fortunately. He hung suspended from the scaffolding until help came, but he never fully recovered from the shock and most of the rest of the work was finished by a pupil, using his sketches. The last 30 ft (9 m) remained blank until 1953 when Allyn Cox added three more panels: the Civil War, the Spanish-American War, and the first flight of the Wright brothers in 1903.

The best of the paintings around the walls are by John Trumbull, showing events in the Revolutionary War in which he actually served. The others are curiosities owing more to the imagination of the artists than to history, or their talents. The middle of the Rotunda's floor is the symbolic center of the city: the street numbers and letters begin with this spot as zero. The bodies of many presidents, former presidents, and other distinguished citizens have lain in state here.

Next to the Rotunda on the south side, **Statuary Hall** groans under a load of bronze and marble versions of famous sons and daughters of the 50 states, sculpted by their local artists. Each state was invited to contribute two, and they responded with good, bad, ugly, and laughable statues; and they're all heavy. The collection now flows out along corridors and down to lower levels, as well. This semicircular chamber was home to the House of Representatives from 1807 to 1857, except while it was being repaired after the British raid of 1814. Look for the plaque in the floor which marks the spot where John Quincy Adams sat, and where he suffered the stroke from which he died. Unique in sitting in the House after serving as president, he is said to have found that the odd acoustics of the room allowed him to eavesdrop on private conversations across the chamber. Stand on the plaque while the guide whispers from the right place. It works.

In the crypt beneath the Rotunda and Statuary Hall, remarkable early photographs taken between 1857 and 1865 show the Capitol with its old dome, no dome at all, and the various stages of construction of the present one. It was originally hoped that George Washington would be buried here, and space was left for a tomb below the crypt, but in his last will, in 1799, he directed that a family vault be built at Mount Vernon. He was laid to rest here, and despite Congressional resolutions, his grand-nephew refused to allow him to be moved.

In the north wing, the earliest part to be built, a high semicircular hall housed the Senate. By 1810 it was split into two levels: the richly elegant upper one, the **Old Senate Chamber**, was modeled on a Greek amphitheater; and the more intimate lower room was the **Old Supreme Court Chamber**. From the latter Samuel Morse sent the first telegraph message, "What hath God wrought," to Baltimore in 1844. In 1860, the Senate having moved to its present quarters, the court shifted upstairs, where it stayed until 1935. Both rooms have been restored to the way they looked in the 1850s. Look at the columns in the small rotunda outside. Instead of the usual acanthus, their Corinthian capitals show New World plants that were a boon to the early American economy—tobacco leaves and corncobs.

You may get a look into the **Senate and House chambers** on a guided tour, if Congress is not in session. But almost everyone who visits Washington wants to see the Senate and the House in action. US citizens can get passes from their senators or representatives by writing ahead of time, or by calling at their offices. Foreign visitors can show their passports (which they are supposed to carry at all times anyway) at the desks of the Sergeant-at-Arms of the Senate or of the Doorkeeper of the House on the upper floor where the gallery entrances are located. There may be a line waiting to get in. The stylish simplicity of the chambers is impressive. The 435 members of the House of Representatives don't have allocated places on the curved rows of benches. The Speaker or a deputy presides. In the smaller Senate chamber, the 100 senators have their own desks arranged in a semicircle, the newest to be elected sitting at the back. The presiding officer here is the vice-president, but he rarely stays after the opening moments (around noon) and a junior senator takes the chair. Prepare to be disappointed with the proceedings. Perhaps only a handful of members will be present, or even just one, droning a tedious speech "for the record." Lively debate is rare in Congress.

In either chamber, you'll see young pages scurrying about on errands for the elect, and congressional reporters in relays recording every word. You'll wait a long time if you want to see history made. Most of the work of Congress, and the real cut and thrust of debate, goes on in committees, which meet in the morning. The public can attend most of them; check the schedule in the day's *Washington Post* under the heading "Today in Congress."

In the basement of the Senate wing, a special open-topped **underground train** runs to the three Senate office buildings north of the Capitol. Take a trip—you're as likely to see a senator on the train as in the chamber.

Walk through the gorgeous gardens to the eastern steps, facing the Mall. From the top, you'll be rewarded with one

Difficult decision-making—this is where the nine justices of the US Supreme Court get down to business.

of the city's best views. At the base stands Washington's finest statuary group, the **Grant Memorial**. This is no triumphant celebration of Civil War victory. The general almost slumps in his saddle, brooding perhaps over the huge losses and miseries that had to be endured first. The flanking groups, cavalry to the north and horse-drawn artillery to the south, convey the desperation and tragedy of battle with poignant drama and realism. If anything, the impact is increased when small children climb up to join the bronze riders. It took the sculptor, Henry Shrady, 21 years to complete the vast composition, and he died, of the strain, it's said, just before it was dedicated in 1922.

Nearby, the **Botanic Garden** (1st Street and Maryland Avenue) is a great steamy greenhouse full of orchids and other exotic species. It's a splendid place to stroll through or to sit and relax in.

Supreme Court

(1st and E. Capitol Streets, NE) The Court is opposite the Senate, in a dazzling marble Classical temple that would have satisfied the most vainglorious of Roman emperors. Finished in 1935, after the death of its architect, Cass Gilbert, it was expected to weather to a less blinding whiteness. It hasn't yet.

The Supreme Court is a remarkable institution: it can tell the president that an act of his, or the Congress that a law it has passed, is illegal, and has the power to overrule either. It is the guardian and interpreter of the Constitution. It decides "what the law is," said John Marshall, chief justice from 1801 to 1835, whose statue dominates the ground floor hallway. The president appoints the justices and chief justice, with Senate approval. They continue until death or retirement, so the effect of an appointment may be felt long after a president has left office; there have been only about 100 justices in the history of the United States, and far fewer chief justices than presidents.

The nine justices file in to begin hearings or to deliver their opinions, promptly at 10am on Mondays, Tuesdays, and Wednesdays, two weeks per month from October through May or June. If you wish to watch the proceedings, it's as well to get in line by 9:30am, and if a case has caught the public eye, even that may be too late.

Should you go to a hearing, you'll be struck by the informality—after the initial ceremonial. The justices rock back in their leather chairs and converse. Legal jargon is at a minimum. Each side in a case is strictly limited to 30 minutes' argument, which may be eaten into by the justices' questions and interventions. When the Court is in recess, short tours of the building include a look into the courtroom. The windows are always curtained—light reflected in from those pristine walls would be too bright, but colored marble columns give the eyes a break. As you leave the building, look up at the pediment over the main entrance. Toga-clad figures here represent actual characters, from Chief Justice Marshall to the architect Gilbert himself.

☛ Library of Congress

(1st Street and Independence Avenue, SE) This started out as a small reference collection for the members of Congress. After it was burned by the British in 1814, Thomas Jefferson sold his 6,487 books to the nation: he needed the money and Congress needed the library. Now with its collection approaching 100 million books, newspapers, maps, films, photographs, and so on, it's the greatest store of knowledge in the world.

Space has always been a problem. Congress held a design competition for a new building in 1873 but then procrastinat-

Unlike your neighborhood branch, the Library of Congress isn't willing to lend its many historic treasures.

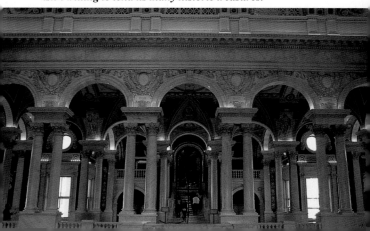

ed for years. They even proposed instead to lift the dome of the Capitol, not long completed after years of effort, in order to insert a library. Finally, in 1897, the building was finished, across Capitol Plaza from the House wing. It's the last word in gorgeous Victorian opulence, and as such was vilified, until quite recently.

Before climbing the great steps, take a look at the animated **Fountain of the Court of Neptune**, with nereids and sea-creatures spurting forth jets of water. The keystones of the second-floor windows are 33 different sculpted heads of racial types from Ainu to Zulu. The **foyer** is jeweled with mosaics, medallions, multicolored marbles, and stained glass, the work of battalions of American artists. A gallery gives a view of the even more palatial octagonal **Reading Room**. Some of the library's greatest treasures on display in the halls include one of three existing copies of the Gutenberg Bible, the first important book to be printed from movable type, Jefferson's draft of the Declaration of Independence, and Lincoln's of the Gettysburg Address. Take a tour to see behind the scenes in the Reading Room, the Thomas Jefferson Building, the newer John Adams Building (1939, Art-Deco, to the east), and the James Madison Memorial Building (1980, without much character, to the south).

Behind the Library of Congress, the **Folger Shakespeare Library** (201 E. Capitol Street, SE) is a monument to the single-mindedness—almost a mania—of a millionaire collector of a uniquely American breed. Henry Clay Folger wasn't born rich, but he rose to become head of the Standard Oil Company of New York (which survives today as the Mobil Oil Corporation). So he gradually became able to indulge a love of the works of Shakespeare that began when he was a student in the 1870s and later shared with his wife Emily, a teacher of English literature. Eventually he bought 79 of the First Folios—

the crown jewels to a Shakespeare collector. He pursued any English book that Shakespeare might have read, too.

Planning a home for his collection, Folger bought land behind the Library of Congress for the building. He saw the cornerstone laid in 1930, but sadly didn't live to see it finished. It's a strange hybrid, but it works beautifully. Outside, a Classical shape with Art-Deco detail and sculptures of Shakespearean characters; inside, an Elizabethan **long hall** for displays of early texts, playbills, and all sorts of stage-related rarities. Don't miss the gem of a **theater**, with its high timber galleries. Plays—not all Shakespeare's—are performed here regularly.

Federal Triangle

The sharp wedge of government buildings between Pennsylvania and Constitution Avenues and 15th Street isn't just for bureaucrats; in the basement of the Department of Commerce, surprisingly, is the **National Aquarium**.

Hungry, hot, or footsore, head for the **Old Post Office** (1899), at the corner of 12th Street and Pennsylvania Avenue, NW. You can get almost anything here except stamps—they're across the street. An emphatic piece of Victorian Romanesque, it doesn't fit the Classical mold of its neighbors; it was only saved from destruction by a vigorous campaign. Now the interior courtyard is a soaring glass-roofed atrium, The Pavilion. Dozens of little shops, restaurants, and fast-food outlets fill the lower levels. You can occasionally see a free lunchtime show on the open stage while you eat your fried chicken, oysters, pasta, curry, hot dogs, or ice cream. Take the glass-sided elevator to the ninth floor and another to the 12th to see the view from the 315-ft (96-m) clock tower, the third tallest structure in the city. Be sure to walk down the stairs past the Congress Bells, replicas of Westminster Abbey's, sent as a bicentenary tribute in 1976.

The original documents of the 1776 Declaration of Independence, the Constitution, and the Bill of Rights are kept in the **National Archives**, at the corner of 9th Street and Pennsylvania Avenue, near the sharp end of the Federal Triangle. The faded treasures are kept in helium gas under green glass now, in contrast to the early years when sightseers could actually handle them. Less noble words can be heard if you take the shuttle bus from outside the Archives to its annex in Alexandria. Here you

Give Ben Franklin a wave when you stop by the Old Post Office for a bite to eat.

can listen to President Nixon and his cronies plotting and cursing on the infamous Watergate tapes.

AROUND THE MALL

Old Downtown

The flight to the suburbs that occurred in most big US cities left their original business and shopping districts shamefully neglected. In Washington, it was the area between the White House and Union Station, a rough diamond enclosed by Pennsylvania, New York, Massachusetts, and Louisiana Avenues. Now it's on the upswing. Real estate like this is too valuable to be left derelict.

Start where Pennsylvania Avenue resumes its progress towards the Capitol after the Treasury. The **Willard Hotel**, once the city's most famous, had fallen on evil days by 1968. Its selling point, "Only a stone's throw from the White House," became an unfortunate phrase in view of the riots that year, and it was boarded up. Now it's back, millions of dollars later, sumptuously restored to turn-of-the-century opulence. Look at the lobby and walk through "Peacock Alley," where all of fashionable society once paraded. The rooftop bar of next-door Washington Hotel gives you the best view in the area.

Across Pennsylvania Avenue, **Pershing Park** beckons visitors with shade, rest, and ducks splashing in a pool that converts to a skating rink in winter. In the middle of the avenue, **Freedom Plaza** is paved with an enormous rendition of L'Enfant's street plan picked out in marble and granite. Some of his manuscript has been reproduced in facsimile: see how he specified the exact widths of sidewalks, gravel walks, and carriageways, and read quotes from famous people about Washington.

Ford's Theater (511 10th Street, NW, between E and F Streets), the scene of Abraham Lincoln's assassination on the night of 14 April, 1865, was closed immediately afterwards and became government offices. Now a National Monument, it was meticulously restored from drawings, photographs, and other records to look exactly as it did on that fateful evening. Since 1968 it has again operated as a theater.

Five days after Lee's surrender at Appomattox sealed the Union victory in the Civil War, President and Mrs. Lincoln and their guests were relaxing in the flag-bedecked box to the right of the stage, watching a comedy, *Our American Cousin,* when the embittered Confederate sympathizer and well-known actor John Wilkes Booth burst in and shot Lincoln. Booth jumped approximately 14 ft (4 m) to the stage, and though he broke a leg in the process, somehow got away. Twelve days later he was himself shot, when troops caught up with him.

Some of the furniture in the box is original, and in the basement there is a **Museum of Lincoln's Life** — and death. Chillingly, you can see the coat, shoes, and gloves he was wearing that night, and Booth's single-shot Derringer pistol.

Lincoln was carried across the street to number 516, the **Petersen House**. Though the White House was scarcely more than half a mile away, the journey over rough and un-paved roads couldn't be risked. In the little bedroom, his 6-ft 4-in (193-cm) frame had to be laid diagonally across the bed. Dr. Charles Augustus Leale, who had been in the audience, probed the headwound and knew there was no hope. The

The agents of the Federal Bureau of Investigation keep tabs on anything suspicious.

president died at 7:22 the next morning. Of the furniture in the house now, only a blood-stained pillow is original.

If the **Federal Bureau of Investigation (FBI)** had existed at the time, its agents would doubtless have been in pursuit of Booth. Visit their headquarters (the entire block between 9th and 10th Streets, E Street and Pennsylvania Avenue, NW), and guides will show you some of their 35,000-gun collection and snow you under with statistics. They do 36,000 fingerprint investigations a day, and half a million computer checks at the request of the forces of law and order around the US and the world. You can examine pictures of the ten most wanted criminals and see if you know one. A honeymoon couple on a tour did—he was their next-door neighbor. You'll get a glimpse of the scientific analysis laboratories and learn what secretors are. The tour finishes with a display of deadly accurate shooting by an agent. Children can ask for the target as a souvenir. The desk for the tour is reached from E Street and there can be a long line waiting. The building is named, naturally, after J. Edgar Hoover, who ran the FBI as a personal fiefdom for 48 years until 1972.

At 901 G Street, the **Martin Luther King Memorial Library** is the only building in Washington from the drawing board of Mies van der Rohe.

To help breathe life into the downtown area, the **Washington Convention Center** was opened in 1983 (between 9th and 11th Streets, NW, New York Avenue and H Street). Hotels and exhibition space have been added since then and the development brought shops and restaurants in its wake. That trend was accelerated by the construction of the **MCI Center** (7th and F Streets NW) in 1997, where Washington's professional basketball and hockey teams play. A colorful archway, a gift of the city of Beijing in 1986, announces DC's own little **Chinatown** (between H and I Streets, NW, from 5th to 8th Streets).

The **Old Pension Building** (F Street, NW, between 4th and 5th Streets) was originally designed to house the administration of pensions for Civil War widows and wounded. Don't be deterred by its dull name: this great brick palace is a stunner. The architect, General Montgomery C. Meigs, was the same engineering genius who finally put the dome on the Capitol. Round the walls is a 1,200-ft- (366-m-) long frieze of terracotta soldiers marching, riding, and rowing boats in endless procession. But it's the vast interior space that takes your breath away. Eight Corinthian columns, the largest ever erected, are each made of 70,000 bricks, plastered and paint-

Washington's magnificent Union Station, restored in the 1980s, is a throwback to the golden era of railway travel.

ed. It was claimed that only a presidential inaugural ball or a thunderstorm could fill the void. There have been many of the first: a thunderstorm has yet to be arranged. Like many one-off buildings of real character, it's often been threatened with demolition, but now as the **National Building Museum** it seems secure from the wrecker's ball.

Union Station

While plenty of their staff scurry to the Metro, not too many members of the Congress these days stroll the half-mile of tree-lined avenue, northeast from the Capitol, to take the train. A pity, because Washington's station is not only a celebration of the railway era, it has been brought back from the dead.

Finished in 1908, its granite entrance recalls Rome's Arch of Constantine. Wise words from the classics are inscribed on its upper panels. In the half-circular plaza in front, Columbus stands in the prow of his ship, looking ahead for land. The soaring parabolic interior was inspired by the Baths of Diocletian—and outdid them.

By the late 1960s, air travel had all but crippled the old railroad companies like the C & O, Richmond, Fredericksburg, and Potomac. Union Station was a leaky mess and the streets nearby were unsafe. Then Congress wasted millions trying to turn the classic building into a Visitor Center for the Bicentennial, spoiling the interior with a labyrinth of partitions. It was a flop. That plan was abandoned and, as part of an effort to clean up and repopulate the east end in its entirety, a major restoration of the station was undertaken in the early 1980s and completed in 1988. Almost all has been restored to its original splendor. Even if you're not taking a train, don't miss the station, its shops, and the basement Food Mall, with multiple fast food and ethnic eating places. There's even a nine-screen movie theater, if you've got a few hours to wait for your connection.

South of the Mall

With the swamps drained and the waters tamed, a half-mile-wide pool, the **Tidal Basin**, was left between the Potomac and the middle of the Mall. You can rent a pedal-powered plastic boat by the hour, which is long enough to see the sights around the banks and probably more than enough for your leg muscles. This would be the ideal way to arrive at the **Jefferson Memorial**, whose Classical portico actually faces the Tidal Basin. A pity then that you have to take the boats back to their pier, but at least pedal over for the view. You can reach it more conventionally: Tourmobile routes come this way as well.

This pristine white tribute to the third president has stood here at the tip of East Potomac Park, practically an island, only since 1943. Its design (by John Russell Pope, the architect of the National Gallery of Art) echoes Jefferson's own Monticello and University of Virginia. The site completes a cross, with the

Capitol, the White House, and the Lincoln Memorial at the other points, and its choice caused the inevitable Washington row. Conservationists bewailed the loss of flowering cherry trees, though surely they'd be consoled now, for in spring the whole area is a mass of blossoms in billowing clouds of pink and white. Architects damned the concept as pompous and cold, dull and imitative, whereas Jefferson was lively, original, and hated excessive ceremony. Time hasn't so much mellowed the building as it has people's reactions to it.

Inside the rotunda, a giant bronze of Jefferson stands 19 ft (5.8 m) tall on a 6-ft (1.8-m) pedestal, but a truer memorial may be found in his words. Some of them are cut into four panels on the walls, with pride of place to phrases from the Declaration of Independence: "We hold these truths to be self-evident, that all men are created equal..." President Kennedy summed up the complex genius that was Jefferson when he called a group of Nobel Prize winners "the most extraordinary collection of talent, of human knowledge, that has ever been gathered together at the White House — with the possible exception of when Thomas Jefferson dined alone."

On the western shore of the Tidal Basin, adjacent to the Jefferson Memorial, is the newest presidential memorial. The 7.5-acre (3-hectare) **Franklin Delano Roosevelt Memorial** is the first fully wheelchair accessible memorial in Washington. Pink granite walls mark off four outdoor "rooms," one for each of his terms in office (1933–1945); the monument is designed so you walk through the rooms in chronological order. Large fountains and waterfalls gurgle, and scattered bronze casts depict Franklin, his wife Eleanor, and Depression-era workers standing in a bread line. Famous quotations ("There is nothing to fear but fear itself") are etched into the walls. Controversy surrounded the dedication in 1997; activists were outraged that—for a place so seemingly accessible to visitors

The Jefferson Memorial is modeled after the Monticello home of the author of the Declaration of Independence.

with disabilities—nowhere in the memorial is Roosevelt (accurately) portrayed in a wheelchair. Since then, Congress has commissioned a new bronze sculpture of Roosevelt in his wheelchair, to be placed at the entrance to the memorial.

To learn how to make money, drop in at the **Bureau of Engraving and Printing** (14th and C Streets, SW). "The buck starts here," proclaim signs on the machines that produce millions of dollars a day in assorted greenbacks, mostly the $1 Washington portrait to replace tired old ones. Security, you'll hardly be amazed to find, is tight, but visitors can walk along glassed-in galleries, looking down on all the operations from blank paper to guillotined stacks worth millions.

NORTH OF THE WHITE HOUSE

The only newspaper to have a Sousa march named after it, the **Washington Post** conducts free tours of its building at 1150

15th Street, NW, at L Street, every Monday (appointments only). Children must be over 11 years old to go on tours. You'll see the vast open newsroom with hundreds of journalists typing frenetically at their VDUs or talking on the phone. All the new technology is on show, along with a display of the way it was in the days of molten lead and noisy linotype machines. Telephone (202) 334-7969 to reserve a place.

The **National Geographic Society's** handsome headquarters (17th and M Streets, NW) houses exhibitions as colorful and professional as its world-reputed magazine. There may be startling laser shows, videos, or a mini-planetarium. **Explorers Hall** presents records and discoveries from expeditions everywhere on earth and in space, with stunning photographs and models. Also, **B'nai B'rith** (1640 Rhode Island Avenue, NW, and 17th Street) has a museum of Jewish life and history in an imposing building here.

Massachusetts Avenue, NW has been called "Embassy Row" ever since foreign diplomats began to take over some of the stately mansions of the rich. Spare a glance for number 1775, the prestigious **Brookings Institution**, concerned with the theory rather than practice of government, a sanctuary where former or future high-level government advisors can do equally high-level research. The group of streets around nearby **Dupont Circle** is the closest thing Washington has to Greenwich Village in New York; bookshops, bike shops, and delicatessens alternate with exclusive clubs. A popular neighborhood for shopping, it's also the focus of much of the city's gay nightlife.

The **Phillips Collection** (1600 21st Street, NW), one of the world's greatest personal art galleries (see page 70), is just off the avenue. Opposite, the **Anderson House** (2118 Massachusetts Avenue, NW) is the palatial home of the Society of the Cincinnati (descendants of Continental officers of the Revolutionary War). The house's interior is overwhelmingly opulent, and is open to the public.

At 23rd and P Streets near the Dumbarton Bridge over Rock Creek to Georgetown, see the dark, moody **statue** of the Ukrainian poet-hero Shevchenko. For more magnificent sculpture, walk to the next bridge, at Q Street, which has four bronze buffaloes that give the 1914 span its name. At **Sheridan Circle** the Civil War general on horseback seems to be waving on the traffic with his hat. Further up Massachusetts Avenue, at number 2551, the **Islamic Center** and mosque impart a flavor of the Middle East. Everyone must remove their shoes before entering—which is no hardship, as the floors are covered with Persian carpets.

Even further up Massachusetts Avenue, the **British Embassy** (notice the Queen-Anne style) is by Sir Edwin Landseer Lutyens.

☞ GEORGETOWN

A little tobacco port stood on the Potomac for over 40 years before the new capital was built next door with the clear intention of eventually gobbling it up. Georgetown, in the District of Columbia from the start, is now governed as part of the big city, but there's no way in which its identity has been submerged. Or, rather, identities in the plural, for Georgetown is quiet, tree-lined streets of little brick or weatherboard houses; gracious mansions in huge gardens; and packed cafés and noisy discos spilling crowds into the streets in the small hours. Sadly, many quaint, small stores have been driven out by the chains, and on evenings and weekends it's maddeningly crowded with pedestrian and street traffic.

Wisconsin Avenue and M Street are the noisy, commercial face of Georgetown, lined with shops and restaurants that may only survive for a matter of months before giving way to the next contender. For contrast, walk in the more tranquil streets east and west of Wisconsin Avenue, where you will often feel as if you're in 18th-century England. Actually, the only pre-Revolutionary house, it is thought, is the solid **Old Stone House** back on M Street. Everything from a goldsmith's to a used car lot in its time, it has been restored to the way it might have looked in the 1770s, complete with guides in costume.

Since rocks and rapids made the Potomac impassable above Georgetown, the obvious thing (before railways) was to cut a canal inland. The rather grandly named **Chesapeake & Ohio Canal** (the "C & O") was started in 1828, but construction stopped in 1850 and it never reached the Ohio River. Abandoned in 1923 and later threatened with being turned into a road, it was restored by 1961 as one of the finest recreational areas that Washington possesses. Its towpath is perfect for cycling or walk-

ing, and you'll see everything from canoes to mule-drawn tour barges on the water. Go as far as you have time for—the whole 184-mile (296-km) length is a national park.

Two of the larger houses on the northern fringe of Georgetown are open to visitors. **Dumbarton House** (2715 Q Street), built about 1800, didn't always stand on the present spot; in 1915 it was moved here on rollers, pulled

Georgetown University buildings are as picturesque as the surrounding village.

You can't forget to visit the zoo—welcoming smiles like this one are guaranteed!

by a horse from its original site 50 ft (16 m) down the hill. Now it holds a fine collection of 18th- and 19th-century furniture and memorabilia of the Washington family. Don't confuse it with **Dumbarton Oaks** (1703 32nd Street, NW). The 1944 conferences that led to the birth of the United Nations took place here. Music-lovers may recall the concerto Stravinsky named after it to mark the 30th wedding anniversary of the owners, Mr. and Mrs. Robert Woods Bliss. Their tastes extended from Byzantine and pre-Columbian art to landscape gardening, and Dumbarton Oaks still houses their collections and libraries (though they were bequeathed to Harvard University). Eight circular glass pavilions by architect Philip Johnson contain Mexican, as well as Central- and South-American, gold and other precious objects. It would be hard to imagine a more perfect setting. The formal gardens are 10 acres (4 hectares) of paradise, terraced above Rock Creek, dotted with pools, a theater, arbors, and statues. The garden gate is at 31st and R Streets. Pick up the map of the gardens, or you'll get lost.

FURTHER NORTHWEST

Like a great slash in the earth, the valley cut by Rock Creek splits Washington into the "northwest" and "The Rest," no matter what street numbers say to the contrary. The tumbling stream can turn into a torrent after rain, and it's vigorous enough to have run several watermills in the old days. **Rock Creek Park** goes all the way from Maryland to the Potomac, more than 10 miles (16 km) by road or track. In places a mile or more across, it narrows to a gorge where bridges cross over to Georgetown. Some of the facilities include separate trails for hikers, bikers, and horseback riders; vestiges of Civil War defenses; picnic areas; an open-air theater; tennis courts; and a public golf course. You can see wheat or oats being ground, and buy a bag of flour at **Pierce Mill** (Beach Drive near Tilden Street), restored after years of standing derelict. The Art Barn next door is a cheerful picture gallery and workshop.

One of the oldest national parks in the world, Rock Creek Park controls 1,800 acres (729 hectares) of green. Most of it is woodland, but the fields are cared for by the "Meadows" program, which has greatly influenced the increase in the diversity of species, whether plants, insects, or birds.

The **Zoo**, as everyone calls the National Zoological Park (3001 Connecticut Avenue, NW), is cleverly laid out along the slopes down to Rock Creek. The environment is already unusually agreeable, but zoos these days have to be sensitive to growing criticism of their role, and this one makes strenuous efforts to be even better. There's green grass instead of cement, and enclosures are open to the sky wherever possible. The animals have their privacy as well, even if it means they're often invisible to the public eye. Trees, shade, and water abound: the river, the hillsides, and the woods make it almost jungle-like in places.

The zoo got its start with animals that were presented to the Smithsonian, which then obtained this site in the leafy suburbs in 1889. Early in the fields of preservation of endangered species and of animal health, this zoo has always been keen to educate visitors. For some reason, the reptile house is built in the style of a Byzantine church. At weekends, study programs for children are "hands-on"—up to a point. In the heat of summer, it's a good idea to go early in the morning (around 8am) if you want to see the animals out-of-doors.

Cathedrals are intended to be seen. With high-rises banned, except for the Capitol and Washington Monument, the **Washington National Cathedral** (Wisconsin and Massachusetts Avenues, NW) stands out more than most, on its 400-foot (122-metre) ridge. It has taken most of the 20th century to build. Perhaps the surprise is not so much the Gothic style, but the authenticity. This is no copy or pastiche: it's one of the biggest cathedrals on earth, but more than that, the same craftsmanship has been devoted to it as to its 14th-century forebears. Notice the stone-carving, the gargoyles, and the flying buttresses (the best view is from the seventh floor in the west end towers). The stained-glass windows are too brilliantly clear to rival Chartres, but here on the south side you'll find one commemorating the 1969 Apollo XI mission to the moon.

Hillwood (4155 Linnean Avenue, NW) is the hidden treasure of the northwest. Even Washingtonians tend to be vague about it. But if you have a chance to see the house and its breathtaking collections, seize it. Ticket prices are only $10 for adults, $8 for seniors, and $5 for students.

Marjorie Merriweather Post bought Hillwood in 1955, already intending that it should eventually be open to the public. She started by collecting French furniture and paintings. Then, when she was in the USSR, she bought artworks that had been confiscated from the aristocracy after the revolution. Eventually she formed the finest collection of Russian decorative arts in the west. You have to join a conducted tour that takes you through rooms packed with a wonderful array of objects. Watch for the masterworks made by the jewelers of the Fabergé workshops, including the famed Easter eggs made for the Imperial family to give each other as presents.

Visitor numbers are strictly limited, so you need to reserve (Tel. 202-686-5807; 877-HILLWOOD, toll-free) not only to see the house but also the grounds, which contain three smaller museums. A Russian-style wooden **Dacha** contains a much smaller Russian collection. A modern log cabin holds Mrs. Post's high-quality American Indian artifacts, and another museum annex houses C. W. Post's mainly Victorian furniture and memorabilia.

It is hard to believe that this splendorous Gothic cathedral was built in the 20th century.

MUSEUMS

Where do you start when offered such a menu? The museum count has reached a dozen on the Mall alone, if you number the components of the Smithsonian separately—as you should—and take the National Gallery of Art's West and East buildings as distinct courses. Don't try to bite off too much in one day, and remember that there are more collections away from the Mall that you may not want to miss.

James Smithson was a British scientist who admired the United States from afar. On his death in 1829 he left over half a million dollars—an incredible sum in those days—

Get your bearings for a day of museum browsing at "The Castle," home to the Smithsonian's visitor's center.

"to found at Washington, under the name of the Smithsonian Institution, an establishment for the increase and diffusion of knowledge among men." Congress debated until 1846 before doing as he wished.

Today, the majority of the museums lining the Mall come under the Smithsonian banner, the main exception being the National Gallery of Art. Most of the museums below (unless otherwise noted) are open every day of the year, except December 25, from 10am to 5:30pm; longer hours may prevail in spring and summer. Amazingly, all of the Smithsonian museums are still free of charge.

The first Smithsonian Institution Building, known as "**The Castle**," is the red sandstone off-balance oddity that sticks out into the Mall looking like a Romanesque church. Finished in

1857, it once contained everything and everyone to do with the institution: now it houses offices, Smithson's tomb, and the Smithsonian Information Center, which opens at 9am. Call (202) 357-2700 with queries on all aspects of Smithsonian activities; (202) 357-2020 for recorded information.

Arts and Industries Building (Smithsonian)

The building houses exhibits from the 1876 Centennial Exposition held in Philadelphia which US and foreign participants gave to the nation—mainly to avoid the expense of shipping them home. After restoration in 1980, the interior again celebrates the colors and style of that time, with many of the original objects on display. You can sense the thrill of new inventions and the pride in the growing industrial power of the United States. *Located between Independence Avenue and Jefferson Drive, SW, at 9th Street.*

Freer Gallery of Art (Smithsonian)

The Freer Gallery is the home of another magnificent array of Oriental art, stamped forever with the fastidious personality of Charles Lang Freer. He laid down the conditions that there could be no loans either from or to "his" museum, nothing could be sold, and very little bought. Although the gallery boasts some of the finest known **Chinese porcelain** and **Islamic painting**, many people go to the Freer primarily to see the famed **Peacock Room**, painted by the American artist James McNeill Whistler, who was a great friend of Freer. Whistler created the Peacock Room for an earlier patron in London to house his ravishing picture *The Princess from the Land of Porcelain*. When Freer bought the room, he had it transported to Washington lock, stock, and barrel. *The Freer Gallery is on Jefferson Drive, SW, at 12th Street.*

☞ Hirshhorn Museum and Sculpture Garden (Smithsonian)

This museum houses the collection formed by Joseph H. Hirshhorn, a man with a mania for art—his kind of art. If he liked it, he bought it. Nobody advised him; he formed perhaps the largest accumulation—4,000 paintings, 2,000 pieces of sculpture—of anyone before or since. Then he gave it to his adopted country, on condition that a museum bearing his name be built. That was in 1966, but he kept on collecting, and when he died in 1981, he left the museum another 6,000 works of art.

Paintings, only a small fraction of the collection at any one time, hang in the windowless (but for one long slit) outer rings of galleries. The bias is towards the modern, adventurous, and American: Avery, Noland, Stella. Nobody likes them all, though most experts agree that Hirshhorn's eye for good sculpture was almost infallible. The pieces are arrayed in the inner rings, bathed in the natural light from the circular courtyard (the hole in the "doughnut"). Look for the little bronzes by artists better known for their painting: Degas, Gauguin, and Matisse, and a witty Picasso, *Woman with Baby Carriage.*

More monumental works are on the plaza outside, and down in the **Sculpture Garden** across Jefferson Drive. It's a perfect setting, with flowering shrubs, fountains, and lawns, for Rodin's colossal *Balzac* and *The Burghers of Calais,* Henry Moore's strange seated figures, and a luscious nude by Maillol. *The Hirshhorn can be entered at Independence Avenue or Jefferson Drive, SW, at 7th Street.*

☞ National Air and Space Museum (Smithsonian)

Heaven has been captured on earth here for anyone who's fascinated by the history of aviation; if you're not that interested, this amazing collection may convert you. The vast foyer on the Mall side is only a foretaste, but none other than the wood and fabric **Wright Flyer** of 1903, which made the first ever powered, manned, controlled flight, hangs in the center spot. It's the original, like all the exhibits, except for some spacecraft that couldn't be returned to earth intact—in which cases the back-up vehicle is displayed. Suspended nearby is Lindbergh's **Spirit of St. Louis**. Only 66 years after the Wright Brothers, the unbelievably compact **Apollo 11 Command Module** brought back the first men to land on the moon.

Tired of all that fine art? Space out at the National Air and Space Museum.

Before you rush to explore the two floors and many galleries full of wonders, check the program of the **Langley Theater**. If you can fit it into your schedule, be sure to see one of the films. Viewing space from earth is the business of the **Planetarium**, so check that program too.

Don't miss Lilienthal's 1894 hang-glider, 70 years before its time (in Gallery 107), World War I (209), World War II (205), and the Golden Age of Flight between the wars (105), with all the right period music and atmosphere. Every gallery is a masterpiece of display. *The Air and Space Museum is entered at Independence Avenue or Jefferson Drive, SW, at 6th Street.*

There's much more in storage at the **Paul E. Garber Facility** in Suitland, outside Washington to the southeast. Over 150 rare planes you probably didn't know still existed are packed so close together in hangars like Aladdin's Cave it's hard to squeeze between them. This site is an extremely popular spot for visitors, so call (202) 357-1400 to make a reservation as far in advance as you can.

National Museum of American Art (Smithsonian)

The NMAA's entrance is dominated by the weird and wonderful *Throne of the Third Heaven* by James Hampton, a revelation in the form of a roomful of objects wrapped in crumpled gold- and silver-colored foil. Among less extraordinary art forms, every era and most schools of American painting are represented chronologically. Find your way to the **Art of the West** gallery: George Catlin and others recorded 1,001 details of Indian life and dress with brilliant realism.

The massive 19th-century Greek revival building (the Old Patent Office) is also home to the **National Portrait Gallery** (8th and F Streets, NW). In the somber halls, row upon row of the famous hang in state: Pocahontas, Morse (a self-portrait), Davy Crockett, Bell, Carnegie, Gertrude Stein, and Tallulah Bankhead by Augustus John, to name a few. Don't try to look at them all, but pick a few themes: the Civil War, the Expanding Frontier, the Twenties. Look for the **Time magazine** cover-portrait collection running from Charles Lindbergh to Raquel Welch, and for **Noguchi's** dramatic sculpted heads. *At 8th and G Streets, NW.*

☛ National Museum of American History (Smithsonian)

This institution has become so lively that some serious minds are a little bit shocked. If it is really "the nation's attic" of the cliché, then the dust has most definitely been swept away; there's some sharp social comment in the exhibitions. Household objects everyone remembers are mounted close to artifacts from the TV era; even J. R. Ewing's hat. A 70-ft- (21-m-) long pendulum in the first-floor lobby demonstrates the earth's rotation by knocking down little pegs in a circle around it. Historic automobiles and locomotives grace the **transport section**.

The second-floor lobby (the Mall entrance) is dominated by a painting of the **Star-Spangled Banner**, a huge copy of the now-tattered original that flew over Fort McHenry near Baltimore in 1814. Still there "in the dawn's early light" after a fierce British bombardment, it inspired Francis Scott Key to write the words of what became the national anthem.

Not at all tattered, various **First Ladies' Gowns** can be seen nearby on vaguely look-alike shop-window models in a copy of the White House's Red Room. The odd, some say absurd, Horatio Greenough **statue of George Washington** half naked in a toga has been an embarrassment, if not a joke, ever since it arrived from Italy in 1841. On the third floor, the real Washington's campaign tent is astonishingly preserved in the **military history section**, as well as the complete gunboat *Philadelphia,* sunk in 1776, raised in 1935. *Entrances on Constitution Avenue and Madison Drive, NW, 12th and 14th Streets.*

National Museum of Natural History (Smithsonian)

This giant magnet for children starts outside with a full-scale fiberglass *Triceratops* for them to climb on, marking the Mall entrance. Go in by that way and you'll encounter a huge stuffed African elephant in the rotunda. Turn right for the **fossil halls** with dinosaur—large and small—skeletons, and life-like models. Dioramas give an idea of everyday life and ceremony in cultures as far flung as Easter Island and Cambodia, and, nearer to home, the American Indians.

Up on the the second floor, the **mineral world** has an encyclopedia of specimens extending to pieces of rock chipped off the moon by astronauts. Don't miss the coldly brilliant jewels in the **Hall of Gems**, with the Hope Diamond, biggest blue diamond known to man and supposed bad luck charm for its owners. Tucked away in a corner on this floor, the **Insect Zoo** is another children's favorite. Here the specimens are alive, in cutaway transparent-sided cases: you can watch bees fly in from the Mall with their loads of pollen and see them crawl right into the hive. *Entrances on Constitution Avenue, at 10th Street, and Madison Drive, 9th to 12th Streets.*

Museums of Asian and African Art (Smithsonian)

The National Museum of African Art and the Arthur M. Sackler Gallery of Asian and Near Eastern Art are joined by a dramatic subterranean concourse called the **International Gallery** which is used for temporary exhibits. The galleries are all below ground.

The **National Museum of African Art** *(950 Independence Avenue, SW)* is the building with six copper domes over its entrance. The stars of this collection are the bronze and brass **castings** from Benin, made with great delicacy, by the ancient lost-wax method. Some are thought to be as much as 600 years old. See, too, the vivid **beadwork** from Cameroon and superb **woodcarvings** and powerful **masks** from Zaire.

You can enter the **Arthur M. Sackler Gallery of Asian and Near Eastern Art** *(1050 Independence Avenue, SW)* through the pavilion with half-a-dozen little pyramids on top. The collection started with yet another of those magnifi-

Discover the origins of man and beast at the Museum of Natural History—always a favorite of the little ones.

cent donations by an enthusiast with money and vision that have so enriched the Washington scene. Dr. Sackler specialized in Chinese **jade** from the dawn of civilization through modern times, Chinese **bronzes**, **paintings**, **lacquerware**, and Near Eastern **metalwork**. Look for the Persian miniatures, so fine that they seem to have been painted with a one-hair brush, and the luxurious **palanquin** from the Japanese Tokugawa period—straight out of *Shogun*.

Corcoran Gallery of Art

"Dedicated to Art," says the apt inscription over the main door of Washington's oldest art museum. Inside, the collection is strong on dramatic **American landscapes**, portraits by John Singer Sargent, and strikingly luminous scenes by Edward Hopper and Winslow Homer. Samuel Morse's documentary *The Old House of Representatives* (1822) didn't impress critics at the time, so he gave up art as a career and became an inventor (the telegraph, the Morse code, etc.). If you like the Pre-

Raphaelites, spare a glance for the French equivalent, a series on the life of Joan of Arc by Boutet de Monval. The Corcoran also exhibits fine glass, tapestries, sculpture, and musical instruments. *New York Avenue and 17th Street, NW; Tel. (202) 639-1700; 800-CORCORAN, toll-free. Open Wednesday–Monday 10am to 5pm, 9pm Thursday. Donation adults $3, families $5.*

☞ National Gallery of Art, West Building

This austere, Classical monument to art is fortunately warmed from within by its brilliant display of wonderful pictures. The building (built in 1941) and the collection owe a lot to Andrew W. Mellon, multi-millionaire of the old school. He gathered the best Old Masters money could buy in the 1920s and 1930s, including some that the hard-up Soviet Union was selling from the Hermitage, and presented them to the nation as the nucleus of a national gallery. Others followed his example: the Dale, Widener, and Kress collections helped fill the new acres of wall space. It's still beautifully uncrowded and admirably lit.

Paintings and sculpture are on the main (second) floor, arranged by country and period; prints, drawings, and decorative arts are on the ground floor. Obtain a plan of the layout from the desk and start from the massive rotunda.

The art of **Florence and Central Italy** (Galleries 1–20) begins with icon-inspired late-Byzantine work. From the Renaissance, Leonardo da Vinci's portrait of the pensive *Ginevra de' Benci* is given pride of place. The only Leonardo in the United States, it's an early work: he was hardly older than his young sitter. Don't miss the vivid portraits by Botticelli, including the rakish *Guiliano de Medici*.

From V**enice and Northern Italy** (Galleries 21–28) come whole rooms of the works of Titian, Tintoretto, and Veronese. Later Italian art, from the 17th and 18th centuries, includes views by Guardi and Canaletto.

The **Spanish Art** collection (Galleries 34–37), although smaller, is of prime quality. Greek-born, Italian-trained El Greco dominates one room with his brilliant colors and attenuated figures. See, too, the honest portrait by Velazquez of *Pope Innocent X,* which caused the subject to sigh *"troppo vero"* ("too true").

The **Flemish and German Paintings** (Galleries 38–45) include the macabre Hieronymus Bosch *Death and the Miser,* showing as he usually did the torments of hell. Rubens is here in every size and a dozen styles to demonstrate his mastery of them all. Sir Anthony van Dyck painted so many English royals and aristocrats that he's often thought of as one himself. You'll see here his portraits of *Charles I* and *Henrietta Maria,* she with her dwarf and monkey.

Dutch Art (Galleries 46–51) includes examples of the genius of Rembrandt, with a penetrating self-portrait from his later life. There's also a chance to see two of the rare works

Despite the name, the fine art at the National Gallery has been acquired from countries throughout the world.

of the enigmatic Jan Vermeer, *Woman with a Balance* and *Woman Writing,* with his magical lighting and air of mystery.

French Art from the 17th to early-19th centuries (Galleries 52–56) features the frothy spontaneity of Jean Honoré Fragonard in *The Swing* and *Blind Man's Buff,* a happy adult game of scarcely veiled eroticism.

The **British Art** collection (Galleries 57–59) includes portraits by Hogarth and Reynolds, Gainsborough's gorgeous *The Honorable Mrs. Graham,* and one of Constable's views of *Salisbury Cathedral.*

American Art (Galleries 60–70) is long on important portraits of early leaders, especially by Gilbert Stuart and Charles Willson Peale, whose son Rembrandt Peale's 1801 painting of his brother Rubens Peale cost a whopping $4 million in 1985. There's an especially American flavor to the later 19th-century work of James McNeill Whistler, even though a lot of his time was spent in Europe. Even more so with Winslow Homer, who took the opposite direction from the Impressionists: he went for clarity of outline and a realism that paradoxically was like no one else's. Look for American scenes by George Bellows, too, such as his *New York* (1911).

Some of the gallery's benefactors specialized in **French Art of the 19th Century** (Galleries 84–92). Two of Monet's studies of *Rouen Cathedral,* half a dozen of the most famous of the Toulouse-Lautrec pictures of raffish Paris life, Renoir's enchanting little *Girl with a Watering Can*—all the great names are here, with some of their most brilliant images represented.

While concentrating on the paintings, don't forget the tapestries, prints and drawings, and furniture and sculpture (especially Daumier's caricatures, *The Deputies*) down in the ground-floor galleries. The treasure-house of a museum shop leads to a concourse connecting the West and East buildings. *Constitution Avenue, NW, between 4th and 6th Streets; Tel. (202) 737-4215. Open Monday–Saturday 10am to 5pm, Sunday 11am to 6pm, except Christmas and New Year's Day. Free admission.*

National Gallery of Art, East Building

Two linked triangular prisms, their edges sharp as knives, somehow present near-symmetrical faces in this building built by I. M. Pei in 1978. Utterly original, it still complements its Classical neighbor, using the same pristine stone. Little glass pyramids, small replicas of the one Pei built at the Louvre in Paris, light the underground walkway between the West and East wings. But try to plan not to go straight from one to the other, so that you don't overdose.

View the apparently limitless space of the interior from all five levels, linked by broad staircases, spiral stairs, escalators, balconies, and elevators. Some of the galleries have special exhibitions, and works from the permanent collection are changed quite often, so each visit is a journey of discovery. You can hope to see some of Picasso's Blue Period, Modigliani's vivid portraits, Jackson Pollock's drip and splash canvases, Mark Rothko's glowing bands of color, and Roy Lichtenstein's giant "comic-book" pictures.

Pick up a program of the free talks and concerts that are frequently held here, especially on weekends. *Pennsylvania Avenue or Madison Drive, entrance on 4th Street; Tel. (202) 737-4215. Open Monday–Saturday 10am to 5pm, Sunday 11am to 6pm, except Christmas and New Year's Day. Free admission.*

National Museum of Women in the Arts

This museum was first in the field when it opened here in 1987 with the aim of celebrating the achievements of female artists. The building is a former male bastion itself, a one-time masonic temple worth seeing in any case for its marble, crystal chandeliers, ceremonial staircases, and exuberant plaster moldings. See the liquid depth of the subjects' eyes in the portraits Elisabeth Vigee-Lebrun painted at the French and Russian courts. Lilla Cabot Perry, a friend of Monet, helped introduce Impressionism to the United States. Her *Lady with a Bowl of Violets* has a compelling, wistful loveliness. *1250 New York Avenue, NW, at 13th and H Streets; Tel. (202) 783-5000. Open Monday–Saturday 10am to 5pm, Sunday noon to 5pm, except Christmas, Thanksgiving, New Year's Day. Donation adults $3, students and seniors $2.*

☛ **Phillips Collection**

In a city of so much art, this is the favorite gallery of many visitors and residents. Duncan Phillips was a boy when his family had this brick-and-brownstone house built. Eventually, he opened it to the public as a showcase for his own wonderful collection of pictures. By 1930, there were so many works of art that he and his wife had to move out. Wings were added, but the feel of a private house remains. Instead of bored guards, there are artists and students to talk to, if you like. Every picture is a jewel of its kind. The vibrant 1901 Picasso *Blue Room* of a girl bathing is lit like a Vermeer. Don't miss Daumier's famous *Three Lawyers* snootily disputing, or the Klee collection, so innovative, funny, and unmistakable, despite his spectrum of styles and materials. If there is one blazing star in this galaxy, it must be the big, exuberant Renoir, *The Luncheon of the Boating Party*. Tear yourself away to see Van Gogh's luminous masterpiece, *The Road Menders,* and the ethereal *Charnel Coast near Dieppe* by Monet. *1600 21st Street, NW, at Q Street; Tel. (202) 387-2151. Open Tuesday, Wednesday,*

Friday, Saturday 10am to 5pm, Thursday 10am to 8:30pm, Sunday noon to 5pm, closed Monday. Admission weekends only, adults $7, students $4.

A Few Special Museums

The Textile Museum is the place to see magnificent rugs and carpets and exhibitions of the world's best embroidery. *2320 S Street, NW; Tel. (202) 667-0441. Open Monday–Saturday 10am to 5pm, Sunday 1 to 5pm. Donation adults $5.*

Children and adults alike will be interested in the **Dolls' House and Toy Museum**. This collection, formed by a zealot, proves that miniaturization didn't begin with the space age. In the late-19th-century heyday of the dolls' house, there was nothing they didn't reproduce in tiny form to fill these small time-capsules of social history. *5236 44th Street, NW; Tel. (202) 244-0024. Open Tuesday–Saturday 10am to 5pm, Sunday noon to 5pm. Admission adults $4, children $2.*

The **Capital Children's Museum** is a "hands-on" kind of place, a rabbit-warren of a former convent that's now the nicest sort of madhouse. Children can lose themselves in a maze, do experiments with light, work with computers, or dress up as fire-fighters and slide down a pole. They can write with quill pens, or run a printing press or a shop of their own. International Hall gives them a glimpse of other cultures—and a taste of the food. *800 3rd Street, NE; Tel. (202) 675-4120. Open daily 10am to 5pm, closed Christmas, Thanksgiving, New Year's Day. Admission $6.*

Anyone drawn to the sea will enjoy the **Navy Yard** on the Anacostia river. You can tour a real destroyer, the *John Barry,* moored just a few blocks from the Capitol, and visit the **US Navy Memorial Museum**, which tells the story of the Navy since the War of Independence. On summer evenings the Navy and the Marines stage free concerts and displays. *7th Street and Pennsylvania Avenue, across from the Archives; Tel. (202) 737-2300, (800) 723-3557. Open Tuesday–Saturday 9:30am to 5pm. Free admission.*

Across the Anacostia from the Navy Yard, the **Frederick Douglass House** overlooks the river from the top of Cedar Hill. The tireless battler for black freedom and civil rights lived here from 1877 until his death in 1895. The area around is now faded, but the house is elegant and filled with the great campaigner's possessions and mementoes of his extraordinary life, from slave to US ambassador. (In summer, the house is on a Tourmobile route.) *1411 W Street, SE; Tel. (202) 426-5961. Open daily 9am to 4pm, until 5pm from April 15 through October 15, closed Christmas, Thanksgiving, New Year's Day. Admission $3, seniors $1.50, children under 6 free.*

 The **United States Holocaust Memorial Museum**, Washington's newest and most moving museum, records the persecution suffered by millions at the hands of the Nazis. After entering through the Hall of Witness, you will be issued a "passport" with the name of a real victim of the Holocaust; then you enter an elevator and are taken up to the museum itself. Artifacts (including a boxcar used to transport prisoners), photographs, films, and eyewitness testimonies make up the permanent exhibition. An account for children ages 8 and above is on the first floor. Though people invariably find the exhibit worthwhile, it is both emotionally and physically taxing. This is one of the most popular attractions in Washington, and admission, though free, is restricted. You must line up and obtain a free, timed ticket. To ensure your admission on a particular day, line up at the ticket window before 9am (though even then you may not be admitted for several hours). Alternatively, you may make a reservation by calling the museum's ticket agency, (Tel. 800-400-9373); be aware that there is a service charge for each ticket reserved.

Potentially the most emotionally distressing museum in all of Washington, the Holocaust Memorial is still a must-see.

You can also purchase tickets directly from the web site <www.tickets.com>. *100 Raoul Wallenberg Place, SW; Tel. (202) 488-0400.*

ARLINGTON

From the Lincoln Memorial, take a favorite joggers' route across the Potomac by the **Arlington Memorial Bridge**, ornamented with massive gilded sculptures. You'll first reach Columbia Island and Lady Bird Johnson Park, planted with a million daffodils and countless flowering trees. Cross the narrow Boundary Channel and you're in Virginia.

The green slopes ahead are still as lovely as in the early days when Martha Washington's grandson, George Washington Parke Custis, chose the hilltop site for his mansion, **Arlington House** (built 1802 to 1817, when the massive Doric portico was finished). His daughter Mary married Robert E. Lee in 1831 and together they lived here for 30 years, whenever army

Arlington Cemetery honors the bravery and discipline of the men and women of the US military.

life permitted. It was in this house that Lee made his decision to refuse the offer of command of Union forces at the outset of the Civil War. Although he supported the Union and opposed slavery, he could not bring himself to fight against his own state. He rode south to Richmond, never to return.

The estate was confiscated and the grounds began to be used for the burial of war dead; out of this grew Arlington National Cemetery. Lee's eldest son fought for the return of his property all the way to the Supreme Court, where he won the case, but now that graves covered the hillsides around the house, he accepted compensation instead of coming back here to live. Recent painstaking restoration and a search for original or similar pre-Civil War furniture now gives an idea of the house in the Lees' day. Also, the guides are dressed up in period costume. Look for the paintings by Custis in the hall and the morning room—he was an accomplished artist.

The vista from the portico was called "the finest in the world" by Lafayette before much of the Washington planned by his compatriot, Pierre L'Enfant, was realized. Today L'Enfant, dismissed amid acrimony at the time, has his tomb just in front of the house, with a perfect view of the city. The granite slab is engraved with his prophetic map.

For many years, all members of the US armed forces and their immediate families could be buried in **Arlington National Cemetery**, but the rate at which space was being used made it necessary to restrict that right, despite the vast area. Near the entrance to Arlington Cemetery stands the new **Women in Military Service for America Memorial**, dedicated in 1997, which honors the more than 1.8 million women who have served in the United States Armed Forces, from the American Revolution to the present. The complex incorporates, once again, a sedate circular reflecting pool, with a semi-circular granite wall framing it from behind. Through arched entryways in the wall, you can go up a staircase and enter the education center, set into the hillside just behind the memorial. (There's a spectacular view of the city and its monuments from up here.) The center details the history of women in the military and houses a database of servicewomen past and present. Its roof is constructed of glass panels, many etched with sayings from famous men and women who served their country.

Walk south on Roosevelt Drive from the memorial to the **Tomb of the Unknown Soldier**. Broad steps climb to a 50-ton (45.5-metric-ton) block of white marble. A single soldier from the US Third Infantry, the oldest formation in the United States, paces to and fro with metronomic precision. Visitors gather on the hour (half-hour in summer) to watch the guard-changing ceremony.

Walk at will under the trees, discovering famous names: Taft, Pershing, John Foster Dulles. It's cool in summer and

The enormous statue of the Marines at Iwo Jima is a familiar Washington image.

bright with blossom in springtime. Make your way back to the slope in front of Arlington House to find the **Kennedy Graves**. An elliptical stone terrace follows the contours of the hill and its wall is incised with words from the 1961 Inaugural Address: "Let the word go forth from this time and place... that the torch has been passed to a new generation of Americans..." Steps climb to a marble terrace where President John F. Kennedy lies below plain flagstones next to his wife Jacqueline Kennedy Onassis. Behind them, an eternal flame flickers. Nearby in the grass, a small white cross and stone mark the grave of the president's brother with the inscription: Robert Francis Kennedy 1925–1968.

The **Pentagon**, headquarters of the US Defense Department, faces the southeast side of Arlington Cemetery, but it's ringed by freeways. The best way to get to it is by Metro, telephoning in advance to reserve a tour (703-695-1776). Allow 30 minutes for completing rigid security checks and bring a passport or international driving license. Be prepared for lots of walking, though the visit only covers about a mile out of the 17 miles (27 km) of corridors. It's tougher on your guide, who keeps up a rapid barrage of facts while walking backwards to see that nobody strays. Along the route you'll pass war art, models of ships and planes, flags and banners, and cases of medals with tales about those who won them. The Pentagon doesn't just have five sides but five stories and five concentric corridors for the five armed services—Army, Navy, Air Force, Marines, and Coast Guard.

The Marine Corps War Memorial, better known as the **Iwo Jima Statue**, is outside Arlington Cemetery to the north. The huge bronze ensemble shows five marines and a sailor raising the Stars and Stripes on Mount Suribachi on 23 February, 1945, during the battle for the Japanese Pacific base of Iwo Jima. It took three more weeks to capture the island and cost 5,000 American lives. Japanese losses were four times higher. The sculpture, based on a famous photograph by Joe Rosenthal, is the work of Felix W. de Weldon and took him nine years. The figures are four times life-size; the whole bronze, at 100 tons (91 metric tons), was the largest ever cast in one piece. The record of past campaigns is written around the base. The flag is raised daily at 8am and lowered at sunset; Marine bands give concerts here in summer.

Elsewhere in Arlington, you'll find the **Newseum** (1101 Wilson Boulevard), the world's first museum devoted exclusively to journalism and the news. Contained within are live video feeds from around the world and multimedia exhibits concerning the history of news gathering and the First Amendment; also on display is a 1455 Gutenberg Bible. The museum sits next to **Freedom Park**, where you'll encounter pieces of the Berlin Wall, a headless statue of Lenin from the final days of the Soviet Union, and the Freedom Forum Journalists Memorial, honoring those killed while in pursuit of a story.

From Arlington, you can return to Washington by crossing the Theodore Roosevelt Bridge, stopping at the **John F.**

Kennedy Center for the Performing Arts (2700 F Street, NW; Tel. 202-416-8000). As late as 1971, when this great complex opened, Washington, DC had no real concert hall or opera house. Suddenly, in one go, there were both, plus two new theaters, the American Film Institute, and much more. The exterior may be massive, but it's hardly beautiful. Intended to be timeless, it is dangerously close to being a dull box.

The inside is a treasury of art—gifts from half the nations of the world. Italy weighed in with 3,700 tons (3,364 metric tons) of Carrara marble, Sweden with Orrefors glass chandeliers, France with Matisse tapestries. Sculptures include works by Epstein and Hepworth, a brilliant bust of Shostakovich by Neizvestny, and the colossal head of Kennedy by Robert Berks. As you'll have come to expect in Washington, there's the usual souvenir shop and guides who will take you on a good tour. Try to come to a performance: there's a spectrum of choices every day of the week. At the least, go up to the rooftop terrace for the superb view—and the cafeteria.

Nearest neighbor to the north is none other than the **Watergate** hotel and apartment complex, where burglars recruited by the wonderfully named CREEP (Committee to Re-Elect the President) broke into Democratic party offices in 1972. It was the attempt by President Nixon and his advisors to cover up these "dirty tricks" that eventually led to his downfall. The multi-layered decorative appearance of the Watergate building has invited the barbed comment that it is a wedding cake, and the Kennedy Center the box in which it came.

EXCURSIONS

Alexandria

Years before Washington was carved out of the Potomac's swampy shore, Alexandria, just 6 miles (10 km) south of

Alexandria, Virginia is noted for its stately historic mansions, such as the Carlyle House, shown here.

Washington in Virginia, was a prosperous port, where clipper-ships could load tobacco. Named after John Alexander, a Scot who arrived in the 17th century, it really began to grow after a town was planned and half-acre lots auctioned in 1749. Lawrence Washington bought one, and his young half-brother George actually drew one of the earliest local street maps.

Part of the area allocated for the District of Columbia, it was returned to Virginia in a Congressional deal in 1846. Today it is part city suburb and dormitory, and looks and feels unmistakably like a town, full of history in its own right. Whether you walk alone or in a group with a costumed guide, or take the "trolley" which is really a bus, pick up a map at the **Ramsay House Visitors Center** (221 King Street; Tel. 703-838-4200).

Actually, Ramsay House is probably older than the town, having long ago been moved by barge along the Potomac

The Stabler-Leadbeater Apothecary Shop filled prescriptions for the forefathers.

from another site. The river then came almost up to this point, and lapped at the bottom of the garden of the neighboring **Carlyle House** (121 N. Fairfax Street; Tel. 703-549-2997). This was, and after restoration is again, one of the finest houses in the town. John Carlyle bought two of the best-placed sections in the 1749 sale and resolved to build in the latest Georgian style from England. The house is on display with painstakingly researched paint colors, varnishes, floor coverings, and furniture. When General Braddock arrived in 1755 to command His Majesty's forces in the French and Indian War and plan the campaign, he did so in Carlyle's house. Fatally wounded only a few weeks later, he still left a poison pill for British rule, for it was his insistence that the colonies pay for their own defense that led indirectly to the American Revolution.

Across from Ramsay House, the old **Stabler-Leadbeater Apothecary Shop** (105-107 S. Fairfax Street; Tel. 703-836-3713), which served the town until 1933, has been preserved with its original furniture. Martha Washington used to send from Mount Vernon for medicines, and Robert E. Lee was in the shop in 1859 when he got his orders to capture John Brown after the raid on Harpers Ferry. Down by the river near the end of King Street, the

Torpedo Factory (105 N. Union Street; Tel. 703-838-4565), after an inspired transformation, houses the galleries, boutiques, studios, and workshops of scores of artists and craftspeople. Tapestry, pottery, painting, and sculpture in every medium, screen-printing, glass engraving, and photography are displayed and in some cases are happening before one's very eyes. One large room has good displays of the archaeology of Alexandria, including bottles and medical bric-a-brac from the Apothecary Shop. If you wish to delve further into Alexandria's history, visit **The Lyceum** at 201 S. Washington (Tel. 703-838-4994); built in 1839, the building has been a library, a Civil War hospital, a home, and an office building, and now houses a museum dedicated to the history of the area and a few galleries as well.

Nearby, at the corner of N. Washington and Cameron Streets (Tel. 703-549-1450), is **Christ Church**, which looks as it did in the late 18th century when George Washington kept a pew here. Robert E. Lee also attended services in his younger days. The boyhood home of Robert E. Lee was located a few blocks away at 607 Oronoco Street, but the Lee family memorabilia, documents, and curiosities are no longer on display here for visitors. Before his father, cavalry general and a hero of the Revolutionary War, moved to the house in 1812, it had seen many visits from George Washington and also the marriage of his wife's grandson. Their daughter later was to marry Robert E. Lee. The house was sold (and closed to the public) at the end of the 20th century. Across the road at number 614, the **Lee-Fendall House** stayed in the family until 1903. It still houses an eclectic collection of antiques and documents (Tel. 703-548-1789).

If you feel sated with old houses, there are plenty of restaurants and shops to visit in Alexandria; or take a seat in the gardens by the river. You can tour a "tall ship" moored near the Torpedo Factory. **Canal Center**, at the north end of town, has a park and a working canal rock.

The curious building, like a stack of diminishing Greek temples, near the King Street Metro station is the 333-ft- (101-m-) high **George Washington Masonic National Memorial** (101 Callahan Drive; Tel. 703-683-2007). Modeled on the Pharos of that other Alexandria in Egypt, the lighthouse that was one of the Seven Wonders of the ancient world, it proudly commemorates the fact that Washington was a mason, and the first master of the Alexandria Lodge number 22. Apart from relics of this connection, you can see the clock from his bedroom which the doctor stopped at the moment of his death, and the family Bible. There's a fine view from the tower, reached by curious elevators or "inclinators" that ride up at a slight angle. As befits a building for, by, and about masons, the structure embodies all sorts of architectural features and symbols. Not all of it is serious. Children will like the mechanical toy parade in one of the first floor rooms.

☛ Mount Vernon

There were those who wished to make the victorious Washington king of the new nation, but he turned them down flat, and looked forward to retirement at Mount Vernon, 16 miles (26 km) south of Washington. On and off, this was his home from 1743 until he died in 1799. You'll soon see why Washington loved it so, but try to arrive early (the gates are open 8am–5pm in the summer and 9am–4pm in the winter; Tel. 703-780-2000).

Washington called himself a "gentleman farmer," but he was an innovative and enterprising one. He was an architect, too: his enlargements at Mount Vernon make it virtually his creation, but he shied away from anything too grand. Restrained dignity and practicality are the keynotes here.

Approach the house by passing the bowling green and trees planted by Washington himself. Inside, you'll notice authentically bright paint; researchers scraped through up to 20 layers to find it. The central hall is a passage from front to back, letting air in during the summer. The key of the Bastille has hung on the wall since 1790 (except when it has been lent for French celebrations), a present from Lafayette for spreading the message of liberty from America to Europe. All the rooms have furniture, paintings, and artifacts of the period, but two have some of George and Martha Washington's actual

The Capitol Columns support a ceiling of blue sky at the National Arboretum.

possessions. Upstairs, their **bedroom** still houses the bed on which he died, of a quinsy (a virulent throat infection) after only two days' illness. It's 6 feet 6 inches (2 meters) long — the general was 6 feet 2 inches (188 cm) tall. Downstairs is his **study** and refuge from all his visitors. Here stand his fine Hepplewhite secretary-desk, his swivel chair, his dressing table, and his globe.

Outside, sit in a chair on the "piazza," a back porch devised by Washington himself, as long as the house and two stories high. Enjoy the view over broad green lawns to the Potomac below before walking through the gardens. Look into the "dependencies" —buildings for cooking, laundering, spinning, and weaving. The workers included some of the 125 slaves employed on the estate (freed, as per Washington's will, a year after his death). The nearby **museum** is full of memorabilia: the bust is a clay origi-

His story has been of great debate, but Thomas Jefferson was an inspirational figure.

nal made by the French sculptor Jean Antoine Houdon in 1785 and the basis of a thousand copies since.

Beyond the stables on the way to the Potomac landing is the **tomb** of George and Martha Washington. Two marble sarcophagi that could hardly be more simply inscribed rest in a brick vault, with relations' and descendants' graves nearby.

National Arboretum

The National Arboretum, 4 miles (6 km) east of downtown Washington (3501 New York Avenue, NE; Tel. 202-245-2726), encompasses 444 magnificent acres (180 hectares) of rolling hills, lakes, woods, and parkland. Springtime is a succession of magnolia, cherry, dogwood, and brilliant azaleas. October brings the fiery reds and golds of autumn foliage. There's always something to admire, whatever the season, from colorful fields of wildflowers to the disciplined bonsai collection.

Monticello

As a young man, Thomas Jefferson cleared a Virginia hilltop near Charlottesville, 105 miles (169 km) southwest of Washington, to build his home, giving it a name that means "little mountain" in Italian. He designed practically every feature of the house himself. Author of the Declaration of Independence, he became

Governor of Virginia, Minister in Paris, then the first Secretary of State in Washington's Presidency, vice-president under John Adams, and himself the third president, from 1801–1809. It was an astonishing career, and Monticello is full of its relics. More than that, the house is marked by the originality of an endlessly inquiring mind. There are countless useful ideas and gadgets.

The setting is idyllic, the "little mountain" rising out of lush landscape. It pays to make the trip early in the day. (Monticello opens 8am–5pm, or 9am–5pm in winter; Tel. 804-984-9800) There's a Visitor Center on Route 20 South near 1-64, a couple of miles away, but that is best visited later, if you decide you want more details of the construction of the house and of daily life in Jefferson's time. Instead of stopping, head straight for Monticello, though you can't drive right to the hilltop. Vehicles have to be parked half a mile away; visitors can ride up in a shuttle minibus or walk. If you pay for your ticket with more than the necessary amount, the cashiers will include in the change a crisp new specimen of the unusual $2 bill—bearing the portrait of Thomas Jefferson.

From the first, Jefferson wanted something quite different from the fashionable "Georgian." He adopted the Palladian style, with a dome inspired by ancient Rome and the first on an American house. Planned for comfort and elegance rather than grandeur, Monticello grew slowly, over a span of 40 years, with many changes incorporated along the way as its owner learned of new inventions—or thought them up for himself. The separate south pavilion was completed first, and it was here that Jefferson lived with his wife Martha in the early years of their marriage. Martha died before he went on his mission to Paris, and it was on his return, full of fresh ideas, that he embarked on the greatest expansion of the house.

You enter through the **East Portico**, where, if you look up, you'll see an indicator that connects to the weathervane on the roof. No need to go outside to check the wind direction. The **Entrance Hall** was a museum even in Thomas Jefferson's day, and more crowded with curios then than now. The antlers of stuffed deer heads were used to hang Indian artifacts brought back by the pioneering Lewis and Clark expedition across the continent, which Jefferson as president had sponsored. The great clock, its single hand still accurate, is propelled by weights. One of them descends past a scale marked with the days of the week, but a hole had to be cut into the floor to accommodate Saturday. A cluster of five rooms in the south wing made up **Jefferson's private quarters**. His bed is in an alcove, or rather an archway, so that he could get out of it on one side into the bedroom, the other into his study.

A plantation house like this needed kitchens, laundry rooms, a dairy, and stables. Instead of housing them in a clutter of outbuildings, Jefferson made use of the slope to conceal them under two L-shaped **terraces**, north and south arms to the house. Walk down to this longer slope to see how the broad eaves gave shade and shelter to the servants and slaves below—and kept them out of sight. Notice the tunnel that goes right through the house, connecting the dependencies and cellars. It is now acknowledged that Jefferson had a years-long affair with one of his slaves, Sally Hemmings; in 1998, tests confirmed that Sally's descendants carry some of Jefferson's DNA.

Thomas Jefferson never stopped experimenting with different plants for his gardens and plantation, which he converted from tobacco to grain. Take time to walk through the grounds: they are a restoration based on Jefferson's records, which of course were meticulous.

You can see how Jefferson wished to be remembered if you walk down to the family **graveyard** and read the words which he himself specified should be written on the obelisk.

Williamsburg

Travel back to the 18th century in Colonial Williamsburg (150 miles/240 km south of Washington), capital of Virginia from 1699 to 1780. Starting in 1926, the philanthropist John D. Rockefeller, Jr. funded the restoration of all the surviving early buildings and reconstruction of the missing ones with meticulous attention to detail and authenticity. You can walk this lively town, where the only wheeled traffic is pulled by horses or oxen. The shops all sell what they might have stocked in colonial times. In workshops and yards you can see the cooper making barrels, and a wheelwright, a gunsmith, and a cobbler at work. They are dressed in period costume and they love answering questions.

The parish church has stood since 1715, but the original 1705 **Capitol** building and the **Governor's Palace** burned down long ago and were rebuilt from the foundations up. Luckily, old prints and drawings were available. The people doing the restoration couldn't have asked for better help with the interior detail: Thomas Jefferson made precise plans when proposing a remodeling of it while he was Governor of Virginia.

Eat in the 18th century, too—Chowning's and Christiana Campbell's taverns and the King's Arms (called the Eagle after the Revolution) date from the 1760s and 1770s. Beautifully restored, they serve authentic and traditional dishes.

Various tickets are on sale at the Visitor Center, covering entry to lists of houses and other buildings. You don't need a ticket to go into the shops or to stroll in the streets. Parking is free at the Visitor Center; pick up a copy of the excellent Visitor's Companion and detailed street map here. Call (800) HISTORY or visit <www.history.org> for more information.

Jamestown, 6 miles (10 km) southwest of Williamsburg on the James River, was settled by pioneers from England in 1607 (13 years before the *Mayflower* reached Massachusetts). Swampy and infested with malaria-carrying mosquitoes, it was not a healthy spot for people, their animals, or their crops. At least 440 out of 500 colonists died between 1609 and 1610. Even so, as Virginia became more prosperous—mainly from cultivating tobacco—Jamestown remained the seat of government for over 90 years, until it moved to Williamsburg. Of the original early buildings, only a church tower still stands.

Just outside the National Park area, in **Jamestown Festival Park**, they've recreated the old three-sided fort, a pottery, and an Indian ceremonial lodge. Off shore float full-size replicas of the three little ships, *Susan Constant, Godspeed,* and *Discovery,* that brought Captain John Smith and the first 103 settlers on their dangerous venture. You can go aboard the *Susan Constant* for a glimpse of what life at sea was like at that time.

The 23 miles (37 km) of the scenic Colonial Parkway from Jamestown via Williamsburg to Yorktown span the entire 174 years of British colonial presence in Virginia. For it was at **Yorktown** in 1781 that Lord Cornwallis surrendered, with his British and German troops effectively sealing the loss of the American colonies. The town today is smaller than it was in the 18th century. Several of the original houses still stand: you can visit the Moore House (Tel. 757-898-2410), where the surrender terms were signed.

Pick up maps at the National Park Visitor Center at the end of Colonial Parkway, where you can view the siege lines from the roof. The battlefield is complicated; before looking around, you may like to see a 25-minute film at the Yorktown Victory Center. For more information about attractions at Jamestown and Yorktown, call (757) 253-4838 or (888) 593-4682.

Annapolis

A miracle of survival and an architectural gem, this small town sits 32 miles (51 km) east of Washington, at the mouth of the Severn River where it flows into Chesapeake Bay. In the half-mile square of the historic center you'll find a hundred charming buildings from the 18th and early 19th centuries. This is a real live community and no precious museum. At either end of East Street stand the **state capitol of Maryland** and the **United States Naval Academy**. Annapolis grew up as a fishing and trading port: today its creeks and inlets are dense with the masts of every kind of leisure craft. The population explodes in summer, as Washingtonians escape onto the water. The best way to see the sights is on foot. Head for State Circle first, and pick up maps and leaflets at the **Old Treasury**, built in 1735.

Baltimore

Maryland's biggest city, 35 miles (56 km) northeast of Washington, was the site of pioneering urban renewal projects, so successful they've been imitated from Boston to San Diego.

Downtown Charles Center breathed new life into the run-down old business district with lively shops, theaters, and cafés. Likewise, the **Inner Harbor** development transformed the once seedy and semi-derelict waterfront into a stylish focus of fun and culture, with dozens of ethnic and seafood restaurants. And don't miss a visit to the **National Aquarium** (Pratt Street on Pier 3; Tel. 410-576-3800), one of the world's best.

Fans of the days of steam can see old locomotives at the **Baltimore & Ohio (B&O) Railroad Museum** (901 Pratt Street at Poppleton; Tel. 410-752-2490). Baseball buffs can go to Babe Ruth's birthplace at **216 Emory Street** (Tel. 410-727-1539).

At **Constellation Dock** on Pier 1 (Tel. 410-539-1797) you can see the restored Navy frigate *Constellation*, launched here in 1797. Take a boat trip to **Fort McHenry**, where successful resistance to a British attack in the War of 1812 inspired Francis Scott Key to write *The Star-Spangled Banner.*

WHAT TO DO

SPORTS

Do-it-yourself exercise will come first for most visitors. Walking, jogging, or running, you'll be in the company of many Washingtonians. You'll find no better arenas than the green expanses of the Mall, Potomac Park, and Arlington, with waterside paths and famous sights along the way. Try Rock Creek Park and the Chesapeake & Ohio Canal towpath, too.

You'll cover even more ground if you rent a bicycle—the ideal method of getting around. Be sure to have a strong lock for when you leave the bike, using it to tie both the frame and wheels to a lamppost or railing. Check in any case that the rental agreement covers the bicycle against damage or theft. You'll see that most riders put on protective headgear and don't care if they do look a little silly.

Few of the central hotels, more of the outer suburban ones, have swimming pools. Otherwise, you face crowds at the public pools or at least an hour's drive to a beach on the Chesapeake Bay, and much further to the ocean beaches of Virginia.

Tennis players will find many public courts. Call (202) 673-7646 to ask about permits to use them. Some of the private clubs will allow visitors to play (see the *Yellow Pages* of the phone book). The same applies to squash and racquetball clubs. Rock Creek Park and East Potomac Park have public golf courses, and there are more out in adjacent Maryland and Virginia. Diplomats and others in the huge foreign community have introduced various exotic sports, sometimes to the stupefaction of the locals. On weekends, in West Potomac Park near the Lincoln Memorial, you might catch a cricket match, or see some rugby, polo, soccer, or softball. Anyone here for the longer term could contact the clubs and join in.

Calendar of Events

The city's broad avenues are made for a parade and hardly a weekend goes by without some sort of ceremonial event. For the big events, dozens of bands and hundreds of floats parade for ten blocks along Constitution Avenue, from 7th to 17th Streets. Some of the main annual occasions are:

February	Chinese New Year, including parade and festivals in Chinatown.
12 February	Lincoln's Birthday; noon ceremony staged at Lincoln Memorial.
22 February/ nearest Mon.	Washington's Birthday Parade 11:30am; ceremony at the Washington Monument.
March	St. Patrick's Day Parade, Constitution Avenue, the Sunday after 17 March, 1pm. Kite Festival, last Saturday in March, held west of the Washington Monument.
March/April	Cherry Blossom Festival; Cherry Blossom Parade, Constitution Avenue, first Saturday in April, 12:30pm. Easter Egg Roll on White House lawn, 10am–2pm Monday after Easter.
4 July	Independence Day fireworks, 9:15pm near Washington Monument. Over the long weekend, Festival of American music and crafts, near the National Museum of American History.
July	Latin-American Festival for a week in early July on Pennsylvania Avenue.
September	Rock Creek Park Festival takes place on a weekend in late September.
Late October	Marine Corps Marathon, 9am, starting from the Iwo Jima Statue and winding through Arlington and DC.
11 November	Veterans' Day ceremony, 11am at the Tomb of the Unknown Soldier.
Mid–late December	Christmas tree lights (Capitol, Ellipse), pageants all over town.

A lone kayaker glides along the water of the Potomac River, a relaxing getaway from the strains of urban life.

This isn't quite the Wild West, but you can ride horses from stables in Rock Creek Park and the suburbs. If you've an urge to get on the water, you can rent a rowboat or canoe on the C & O Canal, sail on the Potomac, go white-water rafting on its rapids, or sedately propel a pedalo on the Tidal Basin near the Jefferson Memorial. More serious sailors will go east to Annapolis to explore the historic waters of the Chesapeake Bay. The renowned Annapolis Sailing School is at 601 6th Street (Tel. 800-638-9192). In a hard winter, the C & O can freeze for skating in a scene like an old Dutch painting; there are also half a dozen indoor rinks where you can rent skates.

Spectator Sports

For longer than anyone can remember, the national games have been baseball and American football, with basketball and ice hockey playing important supporting roles. The seasons for each used to be as fixed as the calendar of the medieval church. Football from September to New Year's Day, baseball from April to October, ice hockey from October to April, and basketball from September to May. Now they are a little blurred at both ends, with pre-season games, play-offs, and various "bowls," but essentially the pattern remains. It's infinitely worth going to a "big game," even if you have no idea of the rules. It's all superbly organized, and a great day out for the whole family.

Washington's own football team, the Redskins, is one of the better teams in the country. They play home games at Jack Kent Cook Stadium in Raljohn, Maryland. Robert F. Kennedy ("RFK") Stadium (East Capitol and 22nd Streets, SE), once home of the Redskins, now hosts Washington's Major League Soccer (MLS) franchise, DC United. The city lost its baseball team to Texas years ago, so you'd have to go to Baltimore to see a major league game. Both the ice hockey (the Washington Capitals) and basketball (the Washington Wizards) teams play at a new downtown arena, the MCI Center. A lot of people prefer watching college games, especially basketball, to the "pro" level, and the universities in and around Washington play some of the best.

No need for a Stairmaster —joggers can get the workout of a lifetime!

SHOPPING

Compare prices and look before you leap in with your credit cards and cash. Sunday's *Washington Post* will give you some idea of what's happening where.

Shopping hours run from about 10am to 6 or 7pm Monday through Saturday, with most suburban, mall, and Georgetown shops opening their doors on Sundays as well. Most department stores are open until 8pm on Thursdays and from noon to 5pm on Sundays.

Where to Shop

Washington, DC has no single area famous for elegant shops. Instead, there are separate concentrations scattered over the city and the inner and outer suburbs. The old downtown area, once blighted, has now been revived, and boasts

Georgetown is the place to spend an afternoon exploring boutique shops.

some of the big-name department stores.

Shopping malls pack the maximum variety of outlets into big, climate-controlled spaces. Downtown, The Shops at National Place (between 13th and 14th, E and F Streets, NW), The Pavilion at the Old Post Office (1100 Pennsylvania Avenue), and Union Station combine varied shopping and eating opportunities even more than most malls. In Georgetown, Canal Square (M and 31st Streets, NW) and Georgetown Park (M Street and Wisconsin Avenue, NW) are multi-level marketplaces of boutiques. The Watergate mall, Les Champs (600 New Hampshire Avenue, NW), has some of the top couturiers at top prices, though those might still be less than on their home turf. Big selections further out of the city include White Flint Mall in Kensington, Maryland, or the two Tysons Corner malls in McLean, Virginia. For "deep discounting," try the biggest with the most, Potomac Mills Mall, sprawling like an airport just off route I-95, 30 miles (50 km) south.

While Georgetown still has its little bookshops, galleries, antiques shops, and boutiques, upscale chain stores have taken over with a vengeance, forcing out many of the more venerable establishments. In fact, the intersection of Wisconsin and M Streets, the neighborhood's ground zero, becomes a veritable parking lot on weekends. Sidewalks are packed five across, making what was once a lovely window-shopping neighborhood significantly more aggravating. Best to come on a weekday morning if you'd like a leisurely browse.

All the art galleries and museums have good gift shops; they're the best place to buy your souvenirs and presents.

What to Buy

Books. With their massive selections, the shops are a pleasure to browse in, and some stay open late. Kramer-Books and Afterwords (1517 Connecticut Avenue, NW) has a bar and café combined. If you are used to fixed prices, sample the big discounts, even on the current best-sellers, at Crown Books and Olsson's. The national chains B. Dalton's and Waldenbooks have branches in some of the shopping malls. Both Barnes & Noble and Borders also have outlets in the city.

Clothes. They've got the lot, somewhere: originals from the Paris salons; some of the best American design at Polo/Ralph Lauren (3222 M Street, NW); trends that caught on and stayed, like the casual and dress-wear at Banana Republic (the corner of M and Wisconsin Streets or 601 13th Street). Most department stores have in-house chic boutiques of big-name designers. There are branches of Benetton and The Limited with trendy looks for women on a reasonable budget. Exciting sportswear is hard to resist, and some casuals cost so little you'd think the fabric alone was worth more.

Crafts. Most souvenirs masquerading as craftwork are mass-produced junk imported from East Asia. For something better, try the museum shops. Look in the Georgetown galleries, too, for genuine handmade Americana. The Department of the Interior Museum (18th and E Streets, NW) has a gift shop that sells American Indian craftwork—new but in traditional styles. For pieces which straddle the boundary between craft and modern art, the Torpedo Factory (105 N. Union Street, Alexandria, Virginia) is a multi-story mall of workshops and outlets (see page 81).

Gadgets. There's always something new in the quest for labor-saving devices, especially to use in the kitchen, the yard (meaning the garden), the pool, or the car. Look in the hardware sections of department stores or in the speciality kitchen shops. (Before buying anything, overseas visitors should make sure that any electrical goods can be adapted to their home voltage and plug system.)

Records. Discounting on CDs is frenetic—just look at the "Weekend" section in the Friday newspapers for the latest sales. When you are shopping around, notice whether you

The Pavilion at the Old Post Office has just about everything the experienced shopper wants—just don't ask for stamps!

are getting a digital recording. Cassettes can be bargains. So can video recordings; but beware, they may not run on your system. Check before you buy.

Stationery. You'll find a delightful array of cards, notepads, and office materials, and the shops are irresistible, with their rainbow-colored displays and frequent new gimmicks.

Wines and spirits. Through some financial wizardry, good French wines can cost less here than in France, but there are no savings on fine California varietals. Discount liquor

Artists and craftspeople of all stripes display their creative efforts at the Torpedo Factory in Alexandria.

stores have specials on spirits that make some prices less than the duty-free shops at the international airports.

ENTERTAINMENT

Visitors here for only a short time need to find out quickly what's going on. Check the newspapers, especially the Friday "Weekend" section of the *Washington Post,* the free *City-Paper* (which appears every Thursday), and *Washingtonian* magazine. Try Ticketplace (at 730 21st Street NW; Tel. 202-

842-5387) for advance or half-price same-day tickets for cultural and sports events.

For news of concerts and lectures, mostly free, at various Smithsonian venues, telephone (202) 357-2700.

When the John F. Kennedy Center's Opera House, Concert Hall, Eisenhower Theater, and half-dozen smaller locations opened, the capital's culture scene was transformed. Now, you may see a pre-New York tryout or a hit play that you missed. World-class ballet companies, touring orchestras, and soloists often include Washington in their itineraries. The Washington Opera performs for a short winter season, and the National Symphony Orchestra, transformed into one of the best in the country by cellist-turned-conductor Mstislav Rostropovitch, gives frequent concerts. Get the *Kennedy Center News* for a full calendar of events.

Look for other concerts—some free—at the Anderson House, Library of Congress, Phillips Collection, Corcoran Gallery, and National Cathedral, to name a few. And you could hardly ask for three locations with more drama than the Elizabethan-style Folger Shakespeare Theater, Ford's Theater, and the restored National Theater.

Where better than the political capital to make capital out of politics? On weekends, satirical cabaret is added to the menu in some bars, restaurants, and clubs such as the Arena Stage (6th Street and Maine, SW).

The choice of movies is vast—check the newspapers. Every suburb has several cinemas but many of the "first run" houses with the latest films are on M Street or Wisconsin Avenue (both the Georgetown end and in the upper northwest). Re-runs and matinees, starting as early as noon, are much cheaper. The American Film Institute at the Kennedy Center shows cult, foreign, and classic films.

Williamsburg isn't known for nightlife, but folks here like to hang out, Colonial-style.

Dancing is offered in bars, clubs, and discos, even afloat the Potomac in a boat. Pick your music from a range of styles as well; the biggest concentration of all varieties is in Georgetown along and near M Street and Wisconsin Avenue, with other pockets on Capitol Hill, near Dupont Circle, and in Alexandria. Note that in the entire US, the minimum legal drinking age is 21. Many clubs make that their minimum entry age as well. Don't expect any real action before 9:30 or 10pm. On weekends, it can be 3am before the crowd starts to thin out.

Jazz fans kept the faith alive through the lean years; now the revival is here and new jazz bars and clubs have joined the long-established Blues Alley (situated behind 1073 Wisconsin Avenue), where you can dine while listening to top performers live. One Step Down (2517 Pennsylvania Avenue, NW) is atmospheric, smoky, and unpredictable.

More sedate and quiet enough for conversation, some of the big hotel bars feature regular pianists and lush surroundings. Men will need a jacket, and probably a tie as well. No such description or restrictions apply to the pubs: at least half of them are Irish, with folk singers and groups to match.

EATING OUT

Eating out is a way of life for many city-dwellers. Yet, not so long ago, Washington could be written off as a gastronomic disaster. Things hadn't advanced much since President Van Buren was rejected by the electorate on suspicion of dining on things foreign and fancy instead of meat, potatoes, and gravy as a good American should. No more. Waves of food fashion have arrived. Better still, waves of immigrants with their own ideas reached the shores of the Potomac and stayed. Now, you can eat a different ethnic cuisine every lunchtime and evening for a month without duplicating. All this competition keeps prices down, too.

You can eat practically around the clock: breakfast blends into lunch, and dinner can start in the afternoon with "early bird" price reductions. Sunday brunches can be gargantuan bargain feasts (sometimes with live musical accompaniment), but you may need to reserve.

The hungry visitor, short of time and funds, will bless that great innovation, the food mall. Dozens of outlets are gathered under one roof, usually with a central area of tables and chairs. Prices are surprisingly low and there's no more than a moment's wait to collect your hamburger, french fries (chips), curry with rice and chapattis, pizza (up to two inches thick), Greek salad, moussaka, hot dogs, sushi, or fried chicken. Health food and salad bars have sprouted everywhere. In some food malls, you select a plateful of salad, which is then weighed at the cash desk; you pay on a per-pound basis. Some of the best-located food malls are: the historic Pavilion at the Old Post Office (Pennsylvania Avenue and 12th Street, see page 42) where lunchtime entertainment is thrown in; The Shops at National Place (13th and 14th, E and F Streets); spectacular Union Station (see page 47); and Crystal City (at the Metro Station).

The Adams-Morgan district, around Columbia Road and 18th Street, NW, is an animated area of multi-ethnic restaurants. Equally, the area around Dupont Circle, at the intersection of Connecticut and Massachusetts Avenues, is a popular spot for dining and evening entertainment.

Fancier restaurants may insist on jackets and ties for men. They can usually lend you something if you arrive without, and you may be glad of it if the air-conditioning is especially fierce.

What to Eat

Washington is a treasure trove of fine restaurants to satisfy every taste and every budget. From the extravagance of Kinkead's to the modest Pasta Mia, high quality food abounds throughout the city. There's also fine people-watching to be done in the city's eateries where the famously powerful and the powerfully famous indulge in conversation over their cuisine.

Fresh fish and shellfish of every variety play a prominent role in Washington's menus. Most comes from the Chesapeake Bay, caught and delivered daily and served at the height of its freshness and flavor. Oysters, scallops, crabs, and clams are especially good and are not to be passed up.

Historic touches from the North and South have found their way onto menus in interesting and delectable ways. Chowders, gumbos, soups, and stews are thick and filling and, more often than not, owe their inspiration to early American cookery. These crowd pleasers can turn up as hearty main courses or "dressed up" and served as fancy starters.

An eclectic selection of scrumptious dessert fare is common in many Washington restaurants. Strawberry shortcake (with baking powder biscuits), key lime pie, interesting variations of cheesecake, and luscious fruit-filled pies are some of the tempting treats featured. Save room for these worthy finales.

Perhaps it seems strange that a visit to the US capital should be one's chance to try Afghan or Ethiopian food. Italian cooking arrived long ago, but became debased into spaghetti and meatballs. Now its focus has sharpened into more authentic and regional dishes. Something similar has happened to the other old-established import, Chinese cuisine. It's still mainly centered in Chinatown (H and I Streets, NW, from 5th to 8th Streets), but instead of just Cantonese modified to early American tastes, customers are demanding and getting genuine dishes from Szechuan, Peking, and Hunan as well.

If the weather is nice, head for an outdoor café in Georgetown for lunch.

Enthusiasm for Thai food has spread around the world; naturally Washington joined in. Restaurants have set up alongside the established French on and off K Street, NW, between 18th and 21st Streets, and others are dotted all over the city. Vietnamese cuisine has also proliferated in Washington over the past few decades, a boon for DC diners. Healthy, light, and appetizing, the food comes in generous portions. If you crave still more variety, there's every kind of Latin American, Middle Eastern, Indian, and dozens of different European restaurants. Nearly always, the cooks have arrived with the cuisine.

HANDY TRAVEL TIPS

An A–Z Summary of Practical Information

A

ACCOMMODATIONS
The Washington, DC Convention and Visitors Association (see Tourist Information Offices) can give you an up-to-date list of hotels, motels, bed-and-breakfasts, and campsites. It's wise to book in advance: the city can be very crowded during convention and holiday periods. You can do this through a travel agent or directly with the hotel. The larger chains have offices in major international capitals and, within the US, toll-free numbers to call (look in the *Yellow Pages* of the telephone directory). In general, you will find that hotel rooms in Washington are not cheap.

Most hotels in Washington, as throughout the US, charge the same price for single or double occupancy. Rates do not normally include taxes. Almost all rooms have air-conditioning, private bathroom, and television. You generally have a choice of twin beds (each may be of double-bed size) or a double bed (dubbed "king" or "queen" depending on size). Children can often sleep in their parents' room without charge, or with a small charge for an extra bed. Room rates do not include any meals unless otherwise stated. The majority of DC hotels (from budget to luxury) offer special weekend, holiday, and off-season rates (up to 50% off business-week rates). Inquire when booking your room.

Bed-and-breakfast. A very popular form of lodging, the term usually stands for moderately priced accommodations in private homes; breakfast is mostly the Continental variety. However, many B&Bs are purpose-built guest houses or inns which operate in a somewhat higher price range. Local tourist brochures often list addresses and telephone numbers for more information.

In Washington, DC, the reservation agencies below cover budget and luxury B&B accommodations both in the city and in Maryland and Virginia suburbs. A booking fee is charged.

Bed 'n' Breakfast Accommodations, Ltd. of Washington, DC, P.O. Box 12011, Washington, DC 20005; Tel. (202) 328-3510; web site <www.bnbaccom.com>.

Bed & Breakfast League-Sweet Dreams & Toast, P.O. Box 9490, Washington, DC 20016; Tel. (202) 363-7767

Washington, DC

Hostels. There are some rooms (or dormitory spaces) in this category in the DC area.

International Guest House, 1441 Kennedy Street, NW, Washington, DC 20011; Tel. (202) 726-5808

Washington International Youth Hostel, 1009 11th Street, NW, Washington, DC 20001; Tel. (202) 737-2333; web site <www.hiwashingtondc.com>.

YMCA, 420 East Monroe Avenue, Alexandria, VA 22301; Tel. (703) 838-8085

Campsites. Several commercial parks operate some distance from the city in Virginia and Maryland, with spaces for vehicles and/or tents. Details are available from the National Parks Service: 1100 Ohio Drive, SW, Washington, DC 20242; Tel. (202) 619-7222

AIRPORTS

Dulles International. Most international flights land at Dulles (IAD), about 28 miles (45 km) west of downtown and 45 minutes away by road (more in rush hour). Express buses and taxis operated by the Washington Flyer cruise between the airport and the city, stopping at several big hotels. There's also a Washington Flyer shuttle-bus service to the West Falls Church Metro station near the Capital Beltway, as well as between Dulles and National airports. The main downtown terminal is at 16th and K Streets next to the Capital Hilton. Call (703) 685-1400 for schedules.

Baltimore/Washington International. Some international airlines headed for Washington, DC use BWI, about 30 miles (48 km) northeast of Washington (9 miles/15 km south of Baltimore), about an hour away by road. Free shuttle buses take passengers to the airport railway station, from where Amtrak and MARC (Maryland Rail Commuter) trains run to Washington's Union Station. In addition to taxis and limousines, it is linked by express buses operated by Super Shuttle, which also has its downtown terminal at 15th and K Streets. Call (410) 761-1689 for information.

National. Most domestic flights use National Airport (DCA), on the Potomac River only 4 miles (6 km) south of downtown Washington and just 10 minutes away by road (20 minutes or more in peak traffic). It is served by taxis, limousines, buses from the terminal at 16th and K Streets, and the Metrorail—there's a free non-stop shuttle-bus service between the terminals and the elevated Metro station.

BUDGETING FOR YOUR TRIP

To give you an idea of what to expect, here's a list of average prices in US dollars. They can only be approximate because of inflation, and because prices vary greatly between one outlet and another.

Airport transfer. Taxi to city center from Dulles $40–42, from National $12–15, from BWI $50–55. By bus to city center from Dulles $16, from National $8, from BWI $13. By Metrorail from National $1.10 (more in rush hour).

Babysitters. $10–12 per hour (professional services), plus transport.

Bicycle rental. $7–22 per day. Deposit or ID required.

Buses. Within DC $1–1.25 (more in rush hour, or into Maryland or Virginia). Exact change required. Children under 5 (two per fare) free.

Car rental. Prices can range from $20 to $55 per day. Shop around and look into weekly rates; benefit from advance reservation, weekend deals, and companies with slightly older, less shiny cars.

Entertainment. Cinema $8–9 (look for cheaper matinées), concerts $10–50, theater $10–50, disco/nightclub/jazz club cover charge $3–10, drinks $3–8.

Hotels (double occupancy, per night; tax not included). Very expensive $250 and up, expensive $200–250, moderate $125–200, inexpensive under $125. Weekend discounts are often available.

Meals and drinks (tax not included). Breakfast $5–12, lunch $5–20, dinner $15 and up, carafe of house wine $10 and up, beer $3–6, spirits $5 and up, soft drinks $1.50, coffee $1.50–3.

Metrorail (underground train). $1.10–$3.25 depending on distance (more in rush hour). Children under 5 (two per paying person) free.

Taxis. No meters; fare depends on zone system. Within one zone, about $3.50 for one person ($1.25 for each additional person), plus $1 for each zone entered.

C

CAR RENTAL

Cars can be rented at the airports and in the city. Charges vary widely, but there's plenty of competition and choice, so shop around. There can be a price advantage in reserving well in advance, before your arrival; it will also help to get the model size you want, and perhaps save a little time when picking it up.

Automatic transmission and air-conditioning are the norm. Note that low-sounding rates can end up much higher when "collision damage waiver" and other extras are added. Check your travel insurance policy to see if you need the "personal/medical" extra: you may be fully covered.

You'll need a valid driver's license and may be asked for your passport (many companies require an International Driving Permit if the renter's national license is in a language other than English). Cash transactions—often refused and generally not accepted for overnight and weekend rentals—may involve cash-deposit application procedures, plus deposits that include the estimated rental charges, as well as a restricted choice of vehicles. If you don't mind a car with the shine off it, find out the rates for older cars from companies with names like "Rent a Wreck" (see the *Yellow Pages*).

Washington, DC is less of a hassle to drive in than many US cities, but parking is still a problem (or expensive) in central areas. Consider getting around by the Metro, buses, taxis, and on foot. A rental car is more useful for the out-of-town excursions and not recommended if you are not planning to leave the city.

WASHINGTON, DC for CHILDREN

The main museums make sure they appeal to all ages. Some, like the National Air and Space Museum, hardly need to try. The Capital Children's Museum is unique: everything is intended to be touched, operated, and used. Some other ideas to consider: the FBI Building; the Dolls' House and Toy Museum; the National Geographic Society's Explorers' Hall; and the National Museum of Natural History, for the dinosaurs and the live Insect Zoo.

Outdoors, there is the Zoo, which organizes special children's activities, Rock Creek Park, and Nature Center (weekends). You can rent pedalos on the Tidal Basin or take a boat trip on the Potomac or C & O Canal. Glen Echo Park (Bethesda, Maryland) holds theater classes for children, as well as free art workshops on Sundays. Kings Dominion theme park, north of Richmond on I-95, is more popular with many children than Colonial Williamsburg, and it's on the way there, or back.

For more ideas and special events, see the Carousel pages of the "Weekend" section of Friday's *Washington Post*.

CIGARETTES, CIGARS, TOBACCO

Cigarettes vary in price depending on where you buy them. A pack from a vending machine costs more than from a newsstand, which in turn is more expensive than a supermarket. Cigarettes are cheaper by the carton of 200. There's an enormous range of pipe tobacco and cigars, though Cuban cigars are not available. Smoking is banned in most public buildings and offices, and in most restaurants. All domestic flights are entirely non-smoking.

CLIMATE and CLOTHING

Climate. Spring, from early April to mid-June, is usually delightful. September and October can be very pleasant. The summer months are hot and humid. Winters are unpredictable: mild or cold, sunny or snowy.

The following chart gives average daily maximum and minimum temperatures in Washington, DC:

In degrees Fahrenheit:

	J	F	M	A	M	J	J	A	S	O	N	D
Maximum	42	44	53	64	75	83	87	84	78	67	55	45
Minimum	27	28	35	44	54	63	68	66	59	48	38	29

And in degrees Centigrade:

	J	F	M	A	M	J	J	A	S	O	N	D
Maximum	6	7	12	18	24	28	31	29	26	19	13	7
Minimum	-3	-2	2	7	12	17	20	19	15	9	3	-2

Clothing. Because many people who come to Washington are here for business, the city may appear more formal than some places, but many residents are much more casual. Still, some restaurants insist on a jacket, tie, or both, especially in the evening, as do some bars. There are discos, surprisingly, that specify "no T-shirts, no athletic shoes, no jeans."

In summer, wear your lightest clothes, cotton rather than synthetics. Because air-conditioning tends to be frigid, you may need another layer to put on when you go inside. In spring and autumn you'll have to be flexible, ready for heat, cold, and rain. Try to catch a weather forecast—they're usually accurate—or dial (202) 936-1212. If you're visiting in winter, be prepared for snow, though it's not guaranteed.

COMMUNICATIONS

Mail. The United States Postal Service (USPS) deals only with mail, in a complicated range of classes. Most post offices are open 8:30am to 5pm Monday through Friday, and some are open on Saturday mornings. The largest city branch (North Capitol Street and Massachusetts Avenue, NE) stays open until midnight Monday through Friday, until 8pm on Saturdays and Sundays. You can buy stamps from machines in many drugstores, airports, etc., at a small surcharge. This is useful, as post offices are rather few and far-between. Mail boxes on the street are blue and easy, at a distance, to confuse with litter bins and newspaper vending machines.

General Delivery (Poste restante). You can have mail marked "General Delivery" sent to you care of the main post office: 900 Brentwood Road, NE, Washington, DC 20066

Letters will be held for no more than a month and may be collected on presentation of your passport or driver's license. Hours are 8am–8pm Mon–Fri, 10am–6pm Saturday and 12pm–6pm Sunday.

Fax. Most big hotels have a fax service for their clients; some even have dataports in each room to which a personal computer or fax machine can be connected. Faxes can also be sent from and received at stationery stores displaying a "Fax" sign, or at such places as Kinko's, which also makes photocopies and rents computers.

Telephone. The telephone system is run by private companies. Pay phones are found in all public places, some accepting coins (25 cents minimum in Washington, DC), some phonecards, and some the major credit cards (foreign affiliates included). Instructions are clearly explained on the machines, and prices listed. When calling long distance, the rules of competition mean that you often have to choose between companies by pushing one button or another; it scarcely matters which to the visitor. Evening (after 5pm) and weekend rates are cheaper. Most airlines, hotel chains, and other big organizations have toll-free numbers beginning with 800 or 888 (dial a 1 first). The toll-free directory can be dialed at 1-800-555-1212.

The area code for DC is 202. Maryland uses 410 and 443, and Virginia uses 703 and 571 for the northern part of the state, 804 for the southern. You must dial the area code if calling from DC to either Virginia or Maryland, or vice versa. However, it is not a long-distance call. To contact the operator, dial 0. For directory information dial 411 within your area code. For other areas dial 1-(area code)-555-1212. Many foreign countries can be dialed direct: see the directory for codes, or dial 0 to ask the operator.

Find out what your hotel charges for telephone calls: it may be considerably cheaper to use a pay phone. If you do, have a pre-paid phone card or plenty of coins ready: an electronic voice may break in to tell you to insert more.

CRIME and THEFT

Since Washington is a government capital, you will find metal detectors at the entrances of all major government buildings and, sadly, at many tourist attractions as well. The best thing to do is cooperate and be patient. In some places, particularly the US Capitol, security has been even more heightened recently.

Travelers to Washington DC should exercise the same cautiousness that they would in any big city. Over the years, the city has had much drug-related crime, but this is almost all confined to parts of the city that you are unlikely to want to go visit. If you take sensible precautions, there's no reason why it should spoil your visit. Store valuables and reserves of cash, travelers' checks, and tickets, etc., in your hotel safe. Keep a separate photocopy of your ticket and passport and a separate record of travelers' check numbers. Carry only what you need from day to day.

Beware of pickpockets, especially in crowds. Make sure your handbag is securely fastened. Keep your wallet in an inside, never a back, pocket. Never leave belongings unattended—or open to view in a car. Leave expensive-looking jewelry at home.

Ask which neighborhoods are unsafe, and keep away from them. After dark, especially, avoid side streets and poorly lit areas. Know where you are going, how to get there and, most important, how to get back.

Lock your hotel room door. When driving through seedier areas, lock the car doors and keep the windows up. Never have attractive items on the seats and the windows open.

If you are robbed, don't put up a fight. Call the police (911) afterward. Obtain a copy of the police report for your insurance company. Report stolen travelers' checks and credit/charge cards as soon as you can.

CUSTOMS and ENTRY FORMALITIES

In general, British visitors with a valid ten-year passport and a return ticket purchased from one of the major airlines do not need a US visa for stays of less than 90 days. Canadian and certain other specified nationals do not need a visa, unless taking employment here. Find out the position from your travel agent, or a US consulate in your home country. If you do need a visa, application forms may be obtained from travel agents, airlines, or US consulates. Allow at least a month for postal applications. If time is very short, you can go in person to the US embassy or consulate. Forms must be accompanied by a passport valid for at least six months longer than the intended visit, a passport-size photograph, evidence of possession of sufficient funds, and proof of intent to leave the United States after the visit. A health certificate is not normally required—check with your travel agent or the issuing embassy/consulate.

Red and green customs channels are in operation at international airports and all formalities are in general more rapid and simple than in the past. If you fly in, the airline should hand you a customs and an immigration form before landing.

The following chart shows certain duty-free items you, as a non-resident, may take into the US (if you are over 21) and, when returning home, into your own country.

Into:	Cigarettes		Cigars		Tobacco	Spirits		Wine
US	200	or	50	or	1,350g	1l	or	1l
Australia	200	or	100	or	250g	1l	or	1l
Canada	200	and	50	and	900g	1.1l	or	1.1l
Ireland	200	or	50	or	250g	1l	and	2l

N. Zealand	200	or	50	or	250g	1.1l	and 4.5l
S. Africa	400	and	50	and	250g	1l	and 2l
UK	200	or	50	or	250g	1l	and 2l

A non-resident may take in articles, free of duty and taxes, up to a value of $100 as gifts. Don't arrive with any plants, seeds, vegetables, fruit, or other fresh food; they're banned. All foods are subject to inspection: it saves time not to take any. Money and checks totaling over $10,000 must be reported.

D

DRIVING

Drive on the right. Provided you stop, check that it's safe, and make sure there are no pedestrians trying to cross, you can turn right at a red light (unless there's a sign to the contrary). The use of seat belts is required in most states, including DC, Maryland, and Virginia. At most circles ("roundabouts") in the US, traffic entering has the right of way. You must stop at least 25 feet (8 meters) away, in either direction on a two-lane road, from a school bus (all yellow) if the driver is flashing red lights, and pass only when the lights are switched off.

Speed limits. Within DC the speed limit is 25 mph (40 km/h). In Virginia and Maryland, on the freeways it is 65 mph (105 km/h); on other roads as marked. You may be surprised at first to find no speed distinction between the lanes on the freeways: all are equally fast, or slow. Certain routes have tidal flow, reversing the direction of lanes or the whole road during rush hours (generally 7–9:30am and 4–6:30pm). Others have commuter lanes which can only be used by vehicles with a stated minimum number of passengers. These restrictions are clearly marked — watch for the signs.

Gas (Petrol) stations are few in the city itself. Some close early and on Sundays. They may require you to pay before filling up, or to have exact change. Note that advertised prices are for self-service; "full serve" can be much more expensive.

Parking is difficult in central Washington, as you might expect. Meters are quickly taken, unless they are limited to 20 or 30 minutes, which wouldn't be much use to most visitors. Don't park where you'll obstruct traffic or you risk being towed away at heavy expense. (If this does happen to you, telephone the Department of Public Works, 202-727-1000.)

Automobile associations. The American Automobile Association, offering information about all kinds of travel, is especially helpful to members of affiliated foreign automobile clubs. Their DC office is at 701 15th Street, NW, Suite 100; Tel. (202) 331-3000. For emergency road service (members only) call 1-800-AAA-HELP.

E

ELECTRIC CURRENT
110-volt 60-cycle A.C. is standard throughout the US. Plugs are the flat, two-pronged (and some three-pronged) variety. Overseas visitors will need a transformer and adapter plug for travel appliances.

EMBASSIES
Just about every country is represented in Washington, DC. Embassies are all located in the northwest of the city, mostly along or near Massachusetts Avenue.

Australia: 1601 Massachusetts Avenue, NW, Washington, DC 20036; Tel. (202) 797-3000
Canada: 501 Pennsylvania Avenue, NW, Washington, DC 20001; Tel. (202) 682-1740
Ireland: 2234 Massachusetts Avenue, NW, Washington, DC 20008; Tel. (202) 462-3939
New Zealand: 37 Observatory Circle, NW, Washington, DC 20008; Tel. (202) 328-4800
South Africa: 3051 Massachusetts Avenue, NW, Washington, DC 20008; Tel. (202) 232-4000
United Kingdom: 3100 Massachusetts Avenue, NW, Washington, DC 20008; Tel. (202) 588-6500

EMERGENCIES
For emergencies, and emergencies only, the all-purpose number (police, fire, ambulance) in the Washington, DC area, as in other major

US cities, is 911. Or dial "0" and tell the operator the number you are dialing from, what kind of help is required, and the address where it is needed. In smaller towns, local emergency numbers are posted on the inside front or back cover of the local telephone directory.

GAY & LESBIAN TRAVELERS

Washington has a lively gay and lesbian scene, mainly in the Dupont Circle, Capitol Hill, and Logan Circle areas; many of the gay and lesbian nightspots are located near Dupont Circle. Both the *Washington Blade* and the *Metro Weekly* (both free) can give the specifics. A good place to start is the Lambda Rising bookstore at 1625 Connecticut Avenue NW (Tel. 202-462-6969), where you can pick up the free weeklies and get some advice.

GUIDES and TOURS

Newcomers to the capital can orient themselves by taking a narrated sightseeing tour—several companies run them. The Landmark Services' Tourmobile Sightseeing buses, authorized by the National Parks Service, take in most major tourist attractions and you can get off and reboard at any stop. There are five different routes, variously including the city, Arlington National Cemetery, Mount Vernon, and the Frederick Douglass home (summer only). The fare naturally depends on your choice—pay when you board or at the booth on the Mall. Contact Tourmobile (Tel. (202) 554-5100; web site <www.tourmobile.com>) for more information. Old Town Trolleys, buses that look like tramcars, also make circuits of the sights and some hotels, with boarding and reboarding permitted. Bus companies run day trips and inclusive overnight packages to the attractions away from Washington, DC, such as Monticello and Williamsburg. Individual licensed guides are available through the Guide Service of Washington, Inc.: 733 15th Street, NW, Suite 1040, Washington, DC 20005; Tel. (202) 628-2842

H

HEALTH and MEDICAL CARE

Free medical service is not available in the US. A visit to a doctor can be expensive; hospitalization a financial disaster. Medical insurance to cover all of your trip is an essential precaution. It can be arranged through an insurance company or agent, or through your travel agent as part of a travel insurance package.

Foreign visitors can ask their embassies in Washington, DC for a list of recommended doctors or can contact the Dental and Physician Referral Service toll-free at 1-800-DOCTORS (362-8677).

Tap water is perfectly safe to drink in the United States.

Drugstores (pharmacies). You may find that some medicines that are obtainable only on prescription in your home country are available over the counter in the US, and vice versa. There are several pharmacies in Washington. The CVS chain has two night branches: 1199 Vermont Avenue, NW; Tel. (202) 628-0720, and 6-7 Dupont Circle, NW; Tel. (202) 785-1466

HITCHHIKING

Except on expressways and parkways, it is legal to hitch, but not advisable. There have been too many cases of assault, robbery, and rape perpetrated by or against hitchhikers. As a result, even the generous Americans are wary. If you try to hitch, you may have some long waits.

HOURS

Most museums are open every day except Christmas Day, but some close on Mondays. Most of the Smithsonian museums are open from 10am to 5:30pm (for information call 202-357-2700).

Shopping hours vary, but are generally from 10am to 5:30 or 6pm Monday through Saturday. Some stores open at noon and close at 7, 8, or 9pm and many, mainly in Georgetown, are open on Sundays from 10, 11am, or noon to 5 or 6pm. Restaurants may close on Sundays or Mondays. Some are open every day of the year. Normal business hours are from 9am to 5pm.

L

LANGUAGE

Even those who think they know all of the most American words and phrases will be constantly taken aback by some new coinage or slang word. People are so incurably inventive. "Divided by their common tongue," English-speakers from other countries can cause confusion and embarrassment. Negotiators had to find out the hard way that "tabling" a motion meant opposite things on the two sides of the Atlantic. And how about the Australian who asked an American if he was "getting a good screw?" (earning a good salary, the Aussie meant).

The following list will help to avoid confusion:

US	British
admission	entry fee
bathroom	toilet
bill	banknote
check	bill (restaurant)
collect call	reverse-charge call
comfort station	public lavatory
detour	diversion
diaper	nappy
divided highway	dual carriageway
elevator	lift
faucet	tap
first floor	ground floor
gas (gasoline)	petrol
general delivery	poste restante
line	queue
liquor	spirits
mail	post
outlet	socket
pants	trousers
rest room	public convenience
round-trip ticket	return ticket
second floor	first floor
stand in line	queue up

Washington, DC

straight	neat (drink)
subway	underground
truck	lorry
trunk	boot (car)
underpass	subway

LAUNDRY and DRY-CLEANING
Hotels may have same-day service and most thoughtfully provide clotheslines in the bathroom, where heating/air-conditioning gives a fast dry. There are numerous quick dry-cleaning shops and coin-operated laundries in the city and suburbs, too.

LIQUOR (ALCOHOL) REGULATIONS
The minimum age for buying (or drinking in public) alcoholic beverages is 21, all over the US. If you look younger than 30, you may be asked to show "some ID" (identification document showing your age).

DC permits the sale of beer, wine, and liquor in a wider range of outlets than many states—in some supermarkets, delicatessens, etc., as well as in liquor stores—and prices are generally as low as or lower than anywhere in the country.

LOST PROPERTY
Each transport system or company has its own lost-and-found department. For the airports, contact the appropriate airport police. Hotels and restaurants normally keep lost items for a few days or weeks in the hope that someone will claim them.

M

MAPS and STREET NAMES
The Washington, DC Convention and Visitors Association and the National Parks Service distribute good free maps and brochures. City and state maps can be purchased in bookstores and gas (petrol) stations.

Whether you walk or ride, you'll soon learn the layout. As a planned city, Washington, DC has a logical pattern. It's divided into quadrants—NW, NE, SE, SW—by North Capitol, East Capitol, and South Capitol Streets and the Mall. North–south streets are numbered, east–west streets have letters, starting at the Capitol. J, X, Y and Z are not used, I streets are sometimes written "Eye," and instead of B streets, there are Independence and Constitution avenues. Other avenues are diagonal to the streets and are named after states.

When the alphabet runs out, names beginning A, B, C, etc., take over, but don't expect total consistency. Physical obstacles often make for dead ends: the very same street may then resume some distance away.

MONEY MATTERS

Currency. The dollar ($) is divided into 100 cents (¢).

Coins: 1¢ (penny), 5¢ (nickel), 10¢ (dime), 25¢ (quarter), 50¢ (half dollar), and $1.

Banknotes (bills): $1, $2 (uncommon), $5, $10, $20, $50, and $100. Larger denominations ($500, $1,000) are not in general circulation. Most denominations are the same size and the same black-and-green color, so be sure to check each one before paying. New editions of the $5, $10, $20, $50, and $100 bills differ from the older versions, with larger portraits on the front and additional coloring. These new bills are in circulation along with the older versions of the same denominations.

It's worth carrying a supply of dimes, quarters, and $1 notes for tips, telephone calls, and small purchases.

For currency restrictions, see Customs and Entry Formalities.

Banks and currency exchange. Banking hours vary, but are typically from 8:30 or 9am to 3pm Monday through Friday. A few banks are open on Saturday mornings. Smaller branches will not change foreign cash. There are exchanges at the airports and in main hotels, but their rates are generally poorer.

Credit and charge cards. "Plastic" money plays an even greater role in the US than in Europe: it's a way of life. The major cards (American Express, Diners Club, MasterCard/Access/Eurocard, Visa and associates, and Discover) are accepted almost everywhere. When paying, you'll often be asked "cash or charge?"

Travelers' checks. You'll find travelers' checks in US dollars drawn on American banks much easier to use, and more often accepted as cash. Only exchange small amounts at a time, keeping the balance in a hotel safe if possible. Keep a record of the serial numbers in a separate place from the checks to facilitate a refund in case of loss or theft.

Washington, DC

Sales taxes. These are added separately to the amount of the bill for your purchases. The general sales tax in Washington, DC is 10% (groceries are free of tax), and in restaurants 10%. Hotels charge a room tax of 13% plus $1.50 per night for "tourism promotion services."

N

NEWSPAPERS and MAGAZINES

The Washington Post and *The Washington Times* are dailies covering the political scene, national and local news, and events. The Friday "Weekend" section of the *Post* has an entertainment guide.

International news is better covered in *The New York Times* and *The Wall Street Journal*. These, and the *London Financial Times,* printed in the US, are sold at newsstands and vending machines.

Look for the free weekly *City Paper* for events, entertainment, and inside stories. The free monthly magazine *Where* is distributed through hotels, and the lively *Washingtonian* carries restaurant reviews and stories about the capital.

Only a few newsstands sell a large selection of foreign papers.

P

PHOTOGRAPHY and VIDEO

All popular brands of film and equipment are available. Look for discount stores, where prices are much lower. There are many same-day color print services. Transparency (slide) film usually takes a few days. It is sold without processing included, which can be a nuisance when you return home.

Airport X-ray machines are of the microdose type, which will not affect ordinary film, but ask for hand-inspection of very high speed film. Lead-lined bags are ineffective. More useful is a lightweight insulating bag to protect film from high temperatures.

Blank video-tape is available for all machines. (Note: pre-recorded tapes made for the US market can't be played on European systems and vice versa; conversion is expensive.)

POLICE

Washington, DC, headquarters of the FBI and CIA, has six police forces. The DC Police, in blue uniforms, look after law and order in the District, and the Metro Transit Police, in brown uniforms, cover security and violations on the Metrobus/Metrorail system only. There are also the US Park Police, US Capitol Police, Uniformed Secret Service, and the Secret Service.

Don't hesitate to ask police officers for assistance or information. Behind their tough image, they're helpful and friendly.

In an emergency, telephone 911 (police, fire, ambulance) in the Washington, DC area or other big cities. In smaller towns, dial "0" for the operator.

PUBLIC (LEGAL) HOLIDAYS

In most states, the following days are public holidays. If a holiday falls on a Sunday, banks and many stores close on the following day. Some Thursday holidays stretch into a long weekend.

1 January	*New Year's Day*
Third Monday in January	*Martin Luther King Day*
12 February	*Lincoln's Birthday*
Third Monday in February	*Washington's Birthday*
Last Monday in May	*Memorial Day*
4 July	*Independence Day*
First Monday in September	*Labor Day*
Second Monday in October	*Columbus Day*
11 November	*Veterans' Day*
Fourth Thursday in November	*Thanksgiving Day*
25 December	*Christmas Day*

R

RADIO and TELEVISION

Few hotel rooms lack a TV set, and few rental cars are without a radio. The choice of channels is vast. The big commercial TV companies fight with each other for the biggest audience, airing predictable formula entertainment and news programs that either repeat themselves endlessly on one issue or chop world events into 25-second bites. For less trivial stuff, and sober news and analysis, try the Public Broadcasting Service (PBS) channel. "The Jim Lehrer News Hour" on PBS gives world as well as national events a better airing.

Radio channels specialize in rock, pop, jazz, country, and other forms of music in various subdivisions. National Public Radio and university-run stations carry more news and classical music.

RELIGIOUS SERVICES
Every conceivable religion is represented in the Washington, DC area—not only the mainstream faiths but countless offbeat and fringe sects. Hotel concierges keep details of the locations and times of major religious services.

T

TIMES and DATES
Washington, DC is in the US Eastern Standard Time Zone, which is five hours behind G.M.T. The clock is advanced by one hour to Daylight Savings Time (G.M.T. minus 4 hours) between the first Sunday in April and the last Sunday in October, dates that are not quite synchronized with European countries. The following chart shows the time in various cities in summer when it is noon in Washington.

L.A.	**Washington, DC**	London	Sydney
9am	**noon**	5pm	2am
Sunday	**Sunday**	Sunday	Monday

For the exact time in Washington, DC, call 844-2525.

Dates in the US are written in the order month/day/year; for example, 1/6/01 means 6 January 2001.

TIPPING
You are expected to add about 15 or 20% to restaurant and bar bills. Even in fast-food establishments and informal coffee shops, Americans sometimes leave a couple of coins on the table. Look carefully before you sign credit/charge card slips in restaurants: they are often left "open" for you to enter a tip. If you do so, fill in the overall total on the bottom line as well. Cinema or theater ushers are not tipped, but door-

men, cloakroom attendants, etc., who have rendered services should be remunerated—not less than $1. Some further suggestions:

Porter	50 cents–$1 per bag (minimum $1)
Hotel maid	$1 per day (not for very short stays)
Lavatory attendant	50 cents
Taxi driver	about 15%
Tour guide	10–15%
Hairdresser/barber	15%

TOILETS

Toilets are referred to by a wide variety of euphemisms: "restroom," "powder room," "bathroom," "ladies' room," or "men's room." There are few public restrooms other than in museums and restaurants, and most will use the internationally recognized pictographs.

TOURIST INFORMATION OFFICES

The United States in general and Washington, DC in particular are well set up with information, leaflets, maps, and lists of events.

Washington, DC Convention and Visitors Association, 1212 New York Avenue, NW, Washington, DC 20005; Tel. (202) 789-7000 for information; web site <www.washington.org>.

White House Visitors' Center, 1450 Pennsylvania Avenue, NW; Tel. (202) 208-1631 for information.

Emergency help for travelers and visitors in need or distress is given by the Travelers Aid Society, located at Union Station; Tel. (202) 371-1937 (branches also at Dulles and National airports).

Visitors from the UK can obtain information prior to arrival, from "Destination USA," 41 Goswell Road, London EC1; Tel. (44) 207 400 7001.

TRANSPORT

WMATA (Washington Metropolitan Area Transit Authority) runs a combined rail (Metrorail) and road (Metrobus) network. Maps are available from some Metro stations and from WMATA, 600 5th Street, NW. Telephone inquiries (202-637-7000) get an informative response, but it may take a while before the call is answered.

Washington, DC

Metrorail rapid transit train system is a revelation to anyone who's used to London's cramped underground or New York's subway. This one is more like Moscow's, without the art. With huge coffered vaults modeled on Rome's Pantheon, the longest escalators in the world, and walls separated from platforms by deep dry moats so they can't be reached by would-be graffiti artists, it's like a set for a science fiction film. The pillar-less design makes for security: there's no place to hide from surveillance cameras. Cleanliness is remarkable —even the carpets (yes, carpets) are vacuumed daily. The cost has reached 11 figures and some lines are still unbuilt: cynics calculate that everyone in DC could have been given a nice car for the money.

Except for Georgetown, nearly everywhere you are likely to visit is within 10 minutes' walk of a Metrorail station. They're marked by discreet (often hard to spot) brown posts capped by an "M." Maps, information, and batteries of ticket machines stand at the bottom end of the escalators. Farecards are needed to enter and exit the system. The machines take coins and banknotes; change is in coins. Select the card value you want. At the end of each trip, the exit gate will stamp the remaining value on it. You can exchange it when you want by feeding it, and more money, into a machine.

Lines are denoted by colors. Trains and platform indicators bear the name of the end-of-the-line destination. The system closes at midnight.

You can switch ("transfer") from the Metrorail to a Metrobus to continue a journey free of charge within DC (for a small surcharge outside). But you must pick up the transfer ticket *before* passing through the Metro entrance gate.

Buses. The Metrobus system is complex. Even the locals don't know all about it. Many bus lines run only in rush hours. Ask your hotel concierge and other travelers at the bus stop to find which line you want. Check with the driver as you get on to ensure you are going the right way. The exact fare is needed, as you put it into a box when you board and drivers don't carry change. Ask for a "transfer" (free) if you are likely to want to continue the journey in the same general direction on another bus. You cannot get a free transfer to a Metro train.

Taxis. There are plenty of cabs, except when it rains. They can be hailed as they pass by, picked up at countless waiting points, or called by telephone (the companies are listed in the *Yellow Pages* under "Taxicabs"). City-based cabs have no meters: the fare depends on a zone system, with a flat rate within one zone and a small surcharge for each extra zone entered. (Additional charges are levied for extra persons, baggage, rush hour, etc.) In less busy streets and rush hours, drivers will stop to pick up extra passengers, but there's no saving on the fare for such a shared ride. Tipping is normal, rounding up the fare by about 15%. Don't expect all taxi drivers to know the city, and especially the suburbs, very well.

TRAVELING TO WASHINGTON, DC

Because of the complexity and variability of the many fares, you need to speak to an informed travel agent well before your date of travel.

By Air

International flights. Most major airlines operate flights to Washington, DC, which is served by three airports (see AIRPORTS).

Apart from standard first class, business/club, and economy fares, main types of fare available are: APEX (book 21 days prior to departure for stays of 7 days to 6 months, no stopovers); Special Economy (book any time, offers plenty of flexibility); Standby (only on the day of travel, generally restricted to summer). Off-season reduced fares and many package deals are also available.

For travelers from Europe, it is occasionally less expensive to buy a round-trip (return) ticket to New York and to continue to Washington, DC by road, rail, or with a domestic airline. However, airline fares have been fluctuating so much recently, it is probably best to consult a travel agent or the Internet.

Domestic flights. There is daily service between Washington, DC and at least one city in every state of the Union, as well as larger Canadian cities. Hourly shuttles operate between Washington, DC and New York or Boston on a first-come, first-served basis. Major destinations are linked with Washington, DC by non-stop flights: the airlines' hub systems necessitate a change of plane before you reach most smaller and more distant places.

Washington, DC

Baggage. You are allowed to check two pieces of baggage of normal size on scheduled transatlantic flights and flights within the United States and Canada. On other international flights the allowance will vary between 44 pounds (20 kg) and 88 pounds (40 kg), depending on what class you are traveling. In addition to checked baggage, one piece of hand luggage that fits easily under the aircraft seat may be carried on board. Check size and weight limits with your travel agent or airline when booking your ticket (which will also show the weight allowance).

It is advisable to insure all luggage for the duration of your trip, possibly as part of a travel insurance package; talk to your travel agent.

By Bus

Major metropolitan centers in North America have regular bus connections with Washington, DC. On normal tickets, the destination must be reached within 60 days after the ticket is purchased. You save about 10% on round-trip (return) tickets. The largest company, Greyhound Trailways Bus Lines, offers rover passes for specified periods of unlimited travel (e.g., 7, 14, or 30 days), but some of these can only be bought outside the US.

You can also take an escorted bus tour to Washington, DC from many places in the Northeast, Midwest, or South.

By Rail

Amtrak trains link Union Station, Washington, DC, with the main cities of the northeast corridor and some in the South. Amtrak's *Metroliner* is a three-hour service between Washington, DC and New York City.

Discount tickets and special package tours are available. If you're planning to travel extensively by train, consider buying regional passes. For information, call 1-800-USA-RAIL. For foreigners, there's the USA Railpass, on sale abroad, and at major railway stations in the US.

W

WEIGHTS and MEASURES

The US is fighting a rear-guard action against the metric system. Milk and fruit juice can be bought by the quart or half-gallon, but wine and spirits come in litre bottles. Food products usually have the weight marked in ounces and pounds, as well as in grams.

Recommended Hotels

The price categories given below are relative; there is no definable high or low season for travel to Washington. In general, count on hotel prices being higher when cherry blossoms are in bloom (late March through early April) and when Congress is in session (mid-September through Thanksgiving and mid-January through June). Also, rates are significantly higher during the week. Contact the hotel directly to see if you can beat their published price; many of the places listed below offer special packages for families, couples, seniors, groups, and government employees that include breakfast and other extras.

Virtually every hotel mentioned here offers a standard roster of amenities: cable TV (often with pay-per-view movies), ironing boards and irons, and hair dryers; most have in-room coffeemakers and safes as well. In most cases, toll-free numbers work in the US only.

Unless otherwise noted, the hotels listed accept major credit cards (American Express, Mastercard, Visa).

$$$$	Above $250
$$$	$200–250
$$	$125–200
$	Below $125

CAPITOL HILL and UNION STATION

Capitol Hill Suites $$ *200 C St. SE; Tel. (202) 543-6000, (800) 424-9165; fax (202) 547-2608; web site <www. politics1.com/chsuites.htm>.* These converted apartment houses, on a residential street across from the Library of Congress, are well-suited for families (continental breakfast included; children under 18 stay free). The one-bedroom accommodations are roomy, with living/dining areas as well as either full kitchens or kitchenettes (there's a market nearby). Décor is pleasant, with mahogany furniture and framed movie posters. 152 suites. Metro: Capitol South.

DOWNTOWN

Capital Hilton $$$–$$$$ *16th St. between K and L Sts. NW; Tel. (202) 393-1000, (800) HILTONS; fax (202) 639-5784.* The site of the annual Gridiron Club Dinner and a comfortable spot. All rooms have writing desks and three separate phone lines (one for computer use). Catch shuttle buses to National and Dulles airports next door. Children stay free. 543 rooms. Metro: Farragut West, Farragut North, or McPherson Square.

Crowne Plaza $$ *14th and K Sts. NW; Tel. (202) 682-0111, (800) 2CROWNE; fax (202) 682-9525.* A warm, pleasant hotel overlooking Franklin Square Park; an excellent bargain. The Beaux-Arts lobby is welcoming, with fresh flowers and plush upholstered furniture. Rooms are decorated in subtle earth-tones and floral prints. Some rooms facing K Street have a view of the Washington Monument. 318 rooms. Metro: McPherson Square.

Grand Hyatt Washington $$$–$$$$ *1000 H St. NW; Tel. (202) 582-1234, (800) 233-1234; fax (202) 628-1641; web site <washington.hyatt.com/wasgh>.* The Grand Hyatt feels like a mini-city; the lobby buzzes with activity. Rooms are done up in shades of tan, with mahogany furniture. A ground-floor deli has a computer with 24-hour internet access. The sports bar is a haven for visiting teams playing at the nearby MCI Center. Children under 18 stay free. 888 rooms. Metro: Metro Center.

Hay Adams $$$$ *16th and H Sts. NW; Tel. (202) 638-6600, (800) 424-5054; fax (202) 638-3803.* Caters to the rich and powerful. Public areas are outfitted with antique furnishings; many guest rooms have silk bedspreads and fine art. For a straight-on view of the White House (one block away), ask for a room facing H Street, from the fifth to the eighth floor. Children under 12 stay free. 136 rooms. Metro: Farragut West or McPherson Square.

Hotel Washington $$–$$$ *15th and Pennsylvania Ave. NW; Tel. (202) 638-5900, (800) 424-9540; fax (202) 638-1595; web site <www.hotelwashington.com>.* The oldest continuously operating hotel in Washington. Rooms have a colonial feel, with blue paisley bedspreads and dark-wood furniture. The top floor terrace/café and restaurant has marvelous views of the Washington Monument. Excellent location. Ask about family discounts; children under 14 stay free. 344 rooms. Metro: Metro Center.

The Jefferson $$$$ *1200 16th St. NW; Tel. (202) 347-2200, (800) 368-5966; fax (202) 223-9039.* A small, ultra-luxurious hotel. Guest rooms are quietly elegant; many boast canopy beds and antique bookcases filled with rare books. Service is discreet, yet unparalleled in attentiveness. The restaurant is lauded as one of the city's best. Children under 12 stay free. 100 rooms. Metro: Farragut North.

Morrison-Clark Inn $$ *Massachusetts Ave. at 11th St. NW; Tel. (202) 898-1200, (800) 332-7898; fax (202) 289-8576.* This lovely, historic inn has charm aplenty. Victorian touches pop up in the common rooms and extend to the guest rooms—lace curtains, carved armoires, and 19th-century engravings. Rates include continental breakfast. Ask about special rates. Children under 12 stay free. 54 rooms. Metro: Metro Center or Mt. Vernon Square.

Renaissance Mayflower $$$$ *1127 Connecticut Ave.NW; Tel. (202) 347-3000, (800) HOTELS-1; fax (202) 776-9182; web site <www.renaissancehotels.com/WASSH>.* Long the venue for presidential inaugural balls (and the one-time home of FDR), this 10-story hotel is on the National Register of Historic Places. Rooms are done up handsomely in mahogany, with ivory and rose accents. Children under 18 stay free. Ask about special summer rates. 565 rooms. Metro: Farragut North.

St. Regis Washington $$$$ *923 16th St. NW; Tel. (202) 638-2626, (800) 325-3535; fax (202) 879-2058.* Sumptuous and elaborate. Rooms are luxurious, with silk-covered walls and alcove "offices" with voice mail and modem hookups. Although just three blocks from the White House, the hotel offers free morning shuttle service anywhere within a 5-mile radius. 193 rooms. Metro: Farragut West or McPherson Square.

Willard Intercontinental Hotel $$$$ *1401 Pennsylvania Ave. NW; Tel. (202) 628-9100, (800) 327-0200; fax (202) 637-7326; web site <hotels.washington.interconti.com>.* The Willard is a Beaux-Arts gem, a restored national landmark that's long been the choice of statesmen (Abraham Lincoln), literary legends (Nathaniel Hawthorne), and a host of foreign leaders. Rooms are spacious and elegant, decorated in Federal style. Children under 18 stay free. 341 rooms. Metro: Metro Center.

FOGGY BOTTOM and GEORGETOWN

Doubletree Hotel Guest Suites $$ *801 New Hampshire Ave. NW; Tel. (202) 785-2000; fax (202) 785-9485.* The Doubletree caters to long-term guests. One-bedroom apartments have living and dining areas and a full kitchen with microwave, range, refrigerator, dishwasher, and china/cutlery. No room service. Located on a quiet residential block around the corner from Kennedy Center. 105 suites. Metro: Foggy Bottom.

Embassy Suites $$ *1250 22nd St. NW; Tel. (202) 857-3388, (800) EMBASSY; fax (202) 785-2411.* This cheerful hotel, built around a 9-story atrium, does a lot of convention and meeting business. Suites have separate bedrooms with brightly colored bedspreads and rosewood furniture, living rooms with sofa beds, and marble baths. Rates include full breakfast and cocktails. 318 suites.

Four Seasons $$$$ *2800 Pennsylvania Ave. NW; Tel. (202) 342-0444, (800) 332-3442; fax (202) 944-2076.* This glamorous Georgetown hotel has hosted everyone from King Hussein to the Irish rock group U2. Rooms are understated yet extravagant, with down comforters, antique framed prints, and plump divans in muted tones. Starlets and regular folks alike get the same friendly, efficient service. Children under 16 stay free. 196 rooms.

Georgetown Dutch Inn $$ *1075 Thomas Jefferson St. NW; Tel. (202) 337-0900, (800) 388-2410; fax (202) 333-6526; web site <www.dchotels.com/dutch.htm>.* Foreign embassy employees and celebrities are frequent guests to this hotel. Offers one- or two-bedroom suites. Rates include continental breakfast and free use of nearby health clubs. Children under 14 stay free. 47 suites.

Holiday Inn Georgetown $–$$ *2101 Wisconsin Ave. NW; Tel. (202) 338-4600, (800) HOLIDAY; fax (202) 338-4458.* One of Washington's best-kept secrets. Located away from the crowds, this chain has well-kept rooms decorated in subtle blue-greys. Rooms on the fifth–seventh floors have lovely views of the Potomac River and Washington Monument. Just a short jaunt downhill from Georgetown's main street. 296 rooms.

The Latham $$ *3000 M St. NW; Tel. (202) 726-5000, (800) 528-4261; fax (202) 295-2003.* Smack in the middle of Georgetown, the Latham has location plus many extras. Higher floor rooms have a view of the river. The small outdoor pool is a bonus. Children under 18 stay free. 97 rooms.

Melrose Hotel $$ *2430 Pennsylvania Ave. NW; Tel. (202) 955-6400, (800) 955-6400; fax (202) 955-5765.* Almost halfway between Georgetown and downtown. The multi-lingual staff (fluent in more than 21 languages) attracts an international clientele. Rooms all have sitting areas; furniture is comfortable, if a bit worn. Ask about special package rates. Children under 18 stay free. 240 rooms. Metro: Foggy Bottom.

Park Hyatt $$$$ *1201 24th St. NW; Tel. (202) 789-1234, (800) 922-PARK; fax (202) 457-8823.* The Park Hyatt is one block from Rock Creek Park, a quiet spot halfway between downtown attractions and Georgetown's shopping and nightlife. Soothing earth tones characterize the rooms; suites have fax machines and sofa beds. Children under 17 free. 223 rooms. Metro: Foggy Bottom or Dupont Circle.

Swissôtel Watergate $$$$ *2650 Virginia Ave. NW; Tel. (202) 965-2300, (800) 424-2736; fax (202) 337-7915.* Not the site of the infamous break-in—that was the adjacent office building. This swank hotel hosts Kennedy Center performers (the complex is next door) and visiting diplomats. Rooms are large, and decorated in French Provincial style. The health club has a lap pool. Children under 17 free. 339 rooms. Metro: Foggy Bottom.

Washington Monarch $$$$ *2401 M St. NW; Tel. (202) 429-2400; fax (202) 457-5010; web site <www.washingtonmonarch.com>.* Take it from Arnold Schwarzenegger—this is the place to come if you want a good workout. The West End Executive Fitness Center, on the hotel's lower level, is an astounding 17,500 square feet. Rooms, many overlooking a manicured interior courtyard, are simple but posh. Children under 18 stay free. 415 rooms. Metro: Foggy Bottom.

ADAMS MORGAN AND DUPONT CIRCLE

Embassy Inn $ *1627 16th St. NW; Tel. (202) 234-7800, (800) 423-9111; fax (202) 234-3309.* This four-story, turn-of-the-century brick inn (no elevator) has modest, comfortable rooms. It's a short walk to both Dupont Circle and Adams Morgan. The Windsor Inn, at 1842 16th St. NW (Tel. 202-667-0300), is under the same management. Rates include continental breakfast, evening sherry and snacks. 38 rooms. Metro: Dupont Circle.

Hotel Sofitel $$$ *1914 Connecticut Ave. NW; Tel. (202) 797-2000, (800) 424-2464; fax (202) 462-0944.* This hotel gets a lot of international business; it's close to most of DC's embassies. Accommodations are roomy, and those on the Connecticut Avenue side have views of downtown. Ask about weekend getaway packages. Children under 12 free. 144 rooms. Metro: Dupont Circle.

Kalorama Guest House $ *1854 Mintwood Place NW; Tel. (202) 667-6369; fax (202) 319-1262.* An inexpensive B&B popular with young people. Quirky and homey—four houses furnished with eclectic antiques. Another branch at 2700 Cathedral Ave. NW (Tel. 202-328-0860). Rates include continental breakfast. 30 rooms (about half of which have private baths). Metro: Woodley Park-Zoo or Dupont Circle.

Radisson Barceló $$ *2121 P St. NW; Tel. (202) 293-3100, (800) 333-3333; fax (202) 857-0134.* Located in a former apartment building, which explains the big rooms—large enough for living alcoves with sofas and desks. Ask about weekend specials. Rooftop pool. Children under 17 stay free. 301 rooms. Metro: Dupont Circle.

Washington Hilton and Towers $$$–$$$$ *1919 Connecticut Ave. NW; Tel. (202) 483-3000, (800) HILTONS; fax (202) 797-5755.* Popular with conventioneers and other groups. Standard rooms; those above the fifth floor have panoramic city views. Children stay free. Outdoor heated Olympic-size pool and tennis courts. 1,118 rooms. Metro: Dupont Circle.

Westin Fairfax $$$ *2100 Massachusetts Ave. NW; Tel. (202) 293-2100; fax (202) 293-0641.* This chic, stately hotel (once the boyhood home of Al Gore) fits in perfectly with the grand mansions along Embassy Row. Rooms are sumptuous, with rich brocade fabrics and marble baths. Rooms on higher floors overlook either Embassy Row or Georgetown. Children under 18 stay free. 206 rooms. Metro: Dupont Circle.

BALTIMORE

Admiral Fell Inn $$–$$$ *888 S Broadway; Tel. (410) 522-7377, (800) 292-4667; fax (410) 522-0707; web site <www.admiralfell.com>.* This appealing inn has served as both a boardinghouse and a vinegar factory. Now, it's a good getaway spot; some rooms have Jacuzzis and canopied beds. Just one block from Baltimore's harbor, in Fells Point, a neighborhood full of boutiques, restaurants, and bars. 80 rooms.

Harbor Court Hotel $$$ *550 Light St.; Tel. (410) 234-0550, (800) 824-0076; fax (410) 659-5925; web site <www.harborcourt.com>.* A charming brick hotel right on the waterfront. Rooms are decorated with antique reproduction furniture; ask for a room facing the harbor. Hamptons, the hotel restaurant, comes highly recommended. 204 rooms.

CHARLOTTESVILLE

Boar's Head Inn $$ *200 Ednam Dr.; Tel. (804) 296-2181, (800) 476-1988; fax (804) 971-5733; web site <www.boarsheadinn.com>.* Run by the University of Virginia, the Boar's Head Inn is a semi-modern facility built around a historic gristmill that houses the inn's tavern and restaurant. Some rooms have fireplaces and views of an adjacent lake. A good jumping-off point for the region's wineries. Tennis facilities on site. The inn also offers hot air balloon rides. 172 rooms.

Keswick Hall $$$–$$$$ *701 Country Club Dr., Keswick, VA; Tel. (804) 979-3440, (800) 274-5391; fax (804) 979-3457; web site <www.keswick.com>.* Keswick succeeds at being an English country inn right in the hometown of Thomas Jefferson (Founding Father of American Independence). Run by Sir Bernard Ashley, this romantic inn is decorated with prints and wallpaper by Laura Ashley (his late wife). The golf course was designed by Arnold Palmer. 48 rooms.

WILLIAMSBURG

Four Points By Sheraton $–$$ *351 York St.; Tel. (800) 962-4743; fax (757) 229-0176.* You can't get much more convenient than this Sheraton, across the street from Colonial Williamsburg and just a short hop from Busch Gardens and the area's golf courses. Suites come equipped with complete kitchen. Indoor pool on premises. Rates include full American breakfast and guaranteed tee times on most area courses. 199 rooms.

Williamsburg Inn $$$$ *136 Francis St.; Tel. (757) 229-1000, (800) HISTORY; fax (757) 220-7096.* Now run by the Intercontinental chain, the Williamsburg is a magnificent Regency-style hotel that looks like an ancestral estate. Foreign leaders and presidents galore have enjoyed the inn's charms. Accommodations are in either the main inn building or one of the adjacent colonial houses and taverns. The golfing here is top-notch. 180 rooms.

Recommended Restaurants

Restaurants are categorized by the average cost of a three-course à la carte meal for one person, excluding drinks, tax, and tip. In general, reservations are recommended. Many of the more expensive restaurants listed below offer more affordable lunch and/or bar menus as well as reasonably priced prix-fixe dinners. Many sightseeing attractions have excellent dining options as well. For instance, the fancy gilt-and-crystal House of Representatives Restaurant in the Capitol (Tel. 202-225-6300) serves breakfast and lunch. And the lovely Café des Artistes at the Corcoran Gallery of Art has an excellent Sunday gospel buffet brunch for $19.95 per person, including drinks (500 17th St. NW; Tel. 202-639-1786).

Unless otherwise noted, restaurants below accept major credit cards (American Express, Mastercard, and Visa).

$$$$	$20–25 (per entree)
$$$	$15–19
$$	$10–14
$	Below $10

CAPITOL HILL and UNION STATION

America **$$** *Union Station, 50 Massachusetts Ave. NE; Tel. (202) 682-9555.* Lunch and dinner daily. This restaurant celebrates the diverse, ethnically influenced cooking of the United States; each dish on the huge menu takes the name of its supposed hometown—the San Antonio (Frito pie), the Peoria (peanut butter and jelly sandwich), etc. Retro murals cover the walls; there's also a good view of the Capitol dome from here. Metro: Union Station.

Barolo Ristorante **$$$$** *223 Pennsylvania Ave. SE; Tel. (202) 547-5011.* Lunch and dinner Monday–Saturday; closed Sunday. Warm and welcoming, Barolo serves elegant northern

Italian food; the menu of meats, fish, and pasta changes often, but try the lobster and fava beans over squid-ink pasta or the asparagus ravioli with sage butter and parmesan. Metro: Capitol South.

B. Smith's $$$ *Union Station, 50 Massachusetts Ave. NE; Tel. (202) 289-6188.* Lunch and dinner daily. An upscale Southern-Creole restaurant; the menu features fried green tomatoes, ribs, jambalaya, and sweet potato-pecan pie. One of the few truly integrated restaurants in the city. Metro: Union Station.

Jimmy T's $ *501 East Capitol St. SE; Tel. (202) 546-3646.* Breakfast and lunch Tuesday–Sunday; closed Monday. An eccentric diner of the old school, with mismatched dishware and a distracted but genial atmosphere. Bring the Sunday paper and linger over traditional artery-clogging American favorites like waffles, omelets, fried eggs, grilled sandwiches, and milkshakes. Expect a line on weekend mornings. Cash only.

Two Quail $$ *320 Massachusetts Ave. NE; Tel. (202) 543-8030.* Lunch and dinner Monday–Friday; dinner only Saturday–Sunday. One of the most romantic spots in the city, decorated in a comfortable hodgepodge of Victorian furniture —even the silver doesn't match. Soft music sets the mood. The food is eclectic American, comforting dishes like stuffed pork chops, grilled chicken, and mesclun salad. Metro: Union Station.

DOWNTOWN

Aroma $$ *1919 I St. NW; Tel. (202) 833-4700.* Lunch and dinner daily. Relaxing Indian restaurant offering the usual curries, tandooris, biryanis, and other Indian dishes, as well as a generous selection of vegetarian items. Great butter chicken.

The $9.95 weekend buffet is an excellent deal. The staff is knowledgeable and helpful. Metro: Farragut West.

Café Atlantico $$$ *405 8th St. NW; Tel. (202) 393-0812.* Lunch and dinner Monday–Saturday; dinner only Sunday. Café Atlantico dishes up snappy island music and inventive Latin American cuisine. Though the menu changes weekly, in general it's Caribbean cooking with a twist. Guacamole is made to order right at your table. Metro: Archives-Navy Memorial.

Café Mozart $$ *1331 H St. NW; Tel. (202) 347-5732.* Open daily. Affordable and authentic, Mozart has it all for the wurst lover—kielbasa, knockwurst, and bratwurst, etc. A casual, homey place where you can pop in for a warm potato soup and some sauerbraten. The lunch specials are an excellent bargain. The beer selection is extensive. Metro: Metro Center.

Capital Grille $$$$ *601 Pennsylvania Ave. NW; Tel. (202) 737-6200.* Lunch and dinner Monday–Friday; dinner only Saturday–Sunday. Steaks are huge, aged in a see-through meat locker. If you're not a serious carnivore, try the sushi-like tuna steak. The wine list is long and impressive. A fairly hip place among young movers and shakers, though a gang of older, cigar-chomping, conservative lobbyists give it the requisite stuffiness. Metro: Archives-Navy Memorial.

Capitol City Brewing Co. $$ *1100 New York Ave. NW; Tel. (202) 628-2222.* Lunch and dinner daily. A brew pub capitalizing on the downtown renaissance. Several different homemade microbrews are on tap, and the menu includes burgers, sandwiches, salads, and fries. The pale-ale chili stands out. There's another branch located across from Union Station that's an after-work hangout for young government staffers. Metro: Metro Center.

Georgia Brown's $$$ *950 15th St. NW; Tel. (202) 393-4499.* Lunch and dinner Monday–Friday; dinner only Saturday; brunch and dinner Sunday. An upscale Southern restaurant that puts a twist on old classics: fried chicken, biscuits and gravy, smothered pork chops, and the like. You'll find several vegetarian choices here as well. Bright and intimate, with comfortable sofa-style booths. Brunch features a jazz trio. Metro: McPherson Square.

Jaleo $$$$ *480 7th St. NW; Tel. (202) 628-7949.* Lunch and dinner daily. This Spanish restaurant/tapas bar fills up at lunch with Capitol Hill staffers. Try the garlic shrimp, red peppers stuffed with goat cheese, and chorizo sticks with garlic mashed potatoes. The paella is huge. No reservations, but the wait's never too long. Metro: Archives or Gallery Place.

Occidental Grill $$$ *1475 Pennsylvania Ave. NW; Tel. (202) 783-1475.* Lunch and dinner daily. This clubby watering hole serves food that is inventive without being weird (swordfish sandwiches and such), but the meat-and-potatoes crowd won't be disappointed, either. Metro: Metro Center, Federal Triangle.

Old Ebbitt Grill $$$–$$$$ *675 15th St. NW; Tel. (202) 347-4801.* Open daily. You might hear the hostess say, "Your table's ready, general," when you're waiting for a seat. But what do you expect of a restaurant established in 1856 just one block from the White House? American cuisine with a seafood bent (try the crabcakes, or oysters from the raw bar). Reservations are a must. Metro: McPherson Square or Metro Center.

Reeves Restaurant and Bakery $ *1306 G St. NW; Tel. (202) 628-6350.* Breakfast and lunch only; closed Sunday. Reeves has been dishing out reliable comfort food since 1886. Go for the old standbys—turkey with gravy or chicken salad with homemade mayonnaise (J. Edgar Hoover's favorite). Save room for the justifiably famous pies. MC, V only. Metro: Metro Center.

FOGGY BOTTOM and GEORGETOWN

Austin Grill $$ *2404 Wisconsin Ave. NW; Tel. (202) 337-8080.* Lunch and dinner daily. Service is snappy (chips and salsa are seemingly bottomless) at this Tex-Mex outpost, and the usual dishes—enchiladas, fajitas, burritos, etc.—are reasonably priced. The crabmeat quesadilla is especially noteworthy. Another branch at 750 E St. NW (near the MCI Center).

Booeymonger $ *3265 Prospect St. NW; Tel. (202) 333-4810.* Open daily. This is the quintessential Georgetown student's hangout. Sandwiches of every type are the focus—try the Manhattan (roast beef, spinach, bacon, and cheddar) or perhaps the Patty Hearst (turkey, bacon, and provolone). Great for a big breakfast.

Burrito Brothers $ *3273 M St. NW; Tel. (202) 965-3963.* Lunch and dinner daily. Probably the best burrito in DC. Value for money is unquestioned—we're talking burritos as big as your forearm. Branches are scattered all over the city.

Kinkead's $$$$ *2000 Pennsylvania Ave. NW; Tel. (202) 296-7700.* Lunch and dinner daily. Perhaps the best seafood restaurant in the city. Chef Bob Kinkead is famous for his complex concoctions, but don't forget the "simple fish," a plain grilled fish which celebrates the fine quality of the seafood. For a light meal and live music, try the downstairs bar.

Old Glory All American Barbecue $$ *3139 M St. NW; Tel. (202) 337-3406.* Lunch and dinner daily. Don't fill up on the biscuits and cornbread; save room for the ribs, brisket, and pulled chicken and pork. Wash it all down with the homemade root beer.

Sequoia $$$ *3000 K St. NW; Tel. (202) 944-4200.* Lunch and dinner daily. This two-story restaurant at Washington Harbor has floor-to-ceiling windows and a huge, terraced patio—all overlooking the Potomac River. Salads and sandwiches to pastas, grilled meats and fish, and pizzas. Metro: Foggy Bottom.

1789 $$$$ *1226 36th St. NW; Tel. (202) 965-1789.* Dinner daily. Located in an elegant two-story Federal townhouse just around the corner from Georgetown University, 1789 is the place to come for a special occasion. The nouveau-American menu changes seasonally. The $29 prix fixe dinner is an excellent deal.

Zed's $$ *1201 28th St. NW; Tel. (202) 333-4710.* Lunch and dinner daily. The most popular of the city's Ethiopian restaurants. Come with a group and share a few combo platters. Worth mention is the *doro watt* (spicy chicken) and *gomen* (collard greens).

ADAMS MORGAN and DUPONT CIRCLE

Food for Thought $ *1831 14th St., NW, Tel. (202) 797-1095.* Dinner Monday–Saturday. Organic food figures prominently in this primarily vegetarian restaurant. Service is nonchalant, so you'll have time to enjoy that coffee or tofu salad. Metro: Dupont Circle.

Kramerbooks and Afterwords Café $ *1517-21 Connecticut Ave. NW; Tel. (202) 387-1462.* Open daily. The place to get dessert and coffee after a night out. Café open 24 hours on weekends. Metro: Dupont Circle.

Nora $$$$ *2132 Florida Ave.; Tel. (202) 462-5143.* Dinner Monday–Saturday; closed Sunday. Rarely is food this healthy so unforgettably delicious. Owner/chef Nora Pouillon strives to use only organic and free-range ingredients. Among her wildly inventive dishes is a couscous risotto with wild mushrooms, spinach, and peppers. MC, V only. Metro: Dupont Circle.

Sam & Harry's $$$$ *1200 19th St. NW; Tel. (202) 296-4333.* Lunch and dinner Monday–Friday; dinner only Saturday–Sunday. All dark wood and deep booths. Folks come for the dry-aged meat and buttery mashed potatoes. Desserts are legendary, especially the chocolate-and-caramel turtle cake. Metro: Dupont Circle.

ALEXANDRIA

Austin Grill $$ *801 King St.; Tel. (703) 684-8969.* Lunch and dinner daily. This branch of the Washington Tex-Mex favorite is equally as colorful, charming, and spicy as the Georgetown original. (see review above).

Gadsby's Tavern $$$–$$$$ *138 N Royal St.; Tel. (703) 548-1288.* Lunch and dinner daily. A throwback to the public houses of colonial times, Gadsby's is a restored late 18th-century tavern that's been turned into a museum, hotel, and restaurant. The pewter plates and glassware befit the era. Offerings include various meat "pyes" and homemade Sally Lunn bread.

BALTIMORE

Obrycki's $$$–$$$$ *1727 E Pratt St.; Tel. (410) 732-6399.* Lunch and dinner daily; closed mid-December to mid-March. You can't come to Maryland without sampling Chesapeake Bay crabs—and Obrycki's has crabs to spare. Order a platter of steamed crab legs. Why bother with anything else?

Paolo's $$–$$$ *301 Light St., Harborplace; Tel. (410) 539-7060.* Lunch and dinner daily. A casual Italian trattoria with a great view of the harbor. The pastas, meat dishes, and salads straddle the line between traditional and creative. Pizzas made in a wood-burning oven come with tasty, offbeat toppings.

CHARLOTTESVILLE

C&O Restaurant $$$ *515 E Water St.; Tel. (804) 971-7044.* Lunch and dinner Monday–Friday; dinner only Saturday–Sunday. An unpretentious yet excellent restaurant, housed in a rustic brick building. Dishes reflect French, Cajun, even Thai influences–and the result is winning. The upstairs dining room is slightly more formal

Silver Thatch $$$ *3001 Hollymead Dr.; Tel. (804) 978-4686.* Dinner Tuesday–Saturday; closed Sunday–Monday. This restaurant, attached to the Inn of the same name, serves elegant New American cuisine. The setting is powerfully romantic. Save room for the chocolate desserts. The domestic wine list is excellent. Reserve ahead; this place is popular.

WILLIAMSBURG

Christiana Campbell's Tavern $$$$ *Waller St.; Tel. (757) 229-2141.* Brunch and dinner Tuesday–Saturday; closed Sunday–Monday. This reconstructed colonial tavern, located within the Williamsburg complex, was a favorite haunt of George Washington. Seafood dishes the specialty. Wandering musicians provide period entertainment. Reserve in advance.

Trellis Cafe, Restaurant, and Grill $$$–$$$$ *403 Duke of Gloucester St., Merchants Square; Tel. (757) 229-8610.* Lunch and dinner daily. Award-winning chef Marcel Desaulniers goes this time for regional American cooking. This nationally acclaimed restaurant is divided into several rooms, each with a different feel. He's written a best-selling dessert cookbook—save room! A popular spot, so reserve well in advance.

INDEX